Local Government in Ohio

SECOND EDITION

CARL M. BROBERG

AMERICAN LEGAL
PUBLISHING CORPORATION
Cincinnati, Ohio

Cover illustration:
The Washington County Courthouse, provided by Robb Harst.

Copyright © 2001 by Carl M. Broberg

All rights reserved. No part of this publication may be reproduced in any form, electronic or mechanical, including photocopy, recording, or any information storage or retrieval system without permission in writing from the publisher.

Library of Congress Control Number: 2001091925

ISBN: 0-9647908-2-3

American Legal Publishing Corporation
432 Walnut Street, 12th Floor
Cincinnati, Ohio 45202
Tel: (800) 445-5588
Fax: (513) 763-3562
E-mail: sales@amlegal.com

Printed in the United States of America

To Daphne . . .
Wife and best friend

Preface

While traveling through the countryside, many years ago in a far away land, an official came upon a woman whose husband had just been eaten by a tiger. She told him that earlier in the year her oldest son had also been eaten by a tiger. The puzzled official asked, "Why don't you move into the city where there are no tigers?"

"But, kind sir," she replied, "there is *government* in the city."

Government lets a few people control the rest of the people. Those who govern make and enforce laws. Government also does things for people that they can't do for themselves. For example, it builds highways and keeps armies. Government is necessary; so why would anyone be afraid of it?

Why? Because in some countries the few who govern treat the rest of the people very badly. The acts of evil governments are recorded in history books and they are reported daily in our news media. A sad fact is that governments can be cruel. The woman who preferred tigers to government must have lived in such a place.

There is a good possibility, but no guarantee, that our country will never become such a place. Our governments (federal, state, and local) can be controlled by the people. However, being able to control and knowing how to control are two quite different things! We cannot control something that is a mystery to us. The purpose of this textbook is to take some of the mystery out of government. If you wonder whether learning about government is worth the effort, remember the tigers.

Contents

Chapter 1: The Three Levels of Government

Introduction 1
   Federal Government and State Government 1
   Local Government 2
   The Impact of Local Government 2
Early Local Governments 3
Federalism 4
   The "Second American Revolution" 4
   The Intended Relationship 5
   The Bill of Rights 6
The Federal-State Relationship Today 8
   The Commerce Clause Versus the Tenth Amendment 8
   The Garcia Case 9
   Recent Commerce Clause Decisions 10
   Federalization 11
The Exercise of Federal Power 11
   Payments 12
   Assurances 12
   Partial Preemptions 13
   Direct Orders 14
   Total Preemptions and Mandates 14
   Chapter 1 Review 15

Chapter 2: Differences on the Local Level

Origin 19
   Counties and Townships 19
   Northwest Territory 20
   Municipalities 22
Home Rule 23
   Municipal Home Rule 24

>   Municipal Laws; Ordinances 24
>   Township Home Rule 25
>   County Home Rule 25
>   Charters 26
>   Municipal Charters 27
>   County Charters 28
>   Direct Democracy 28
>   The Initiative and Referendum 29
>   Enacting and Repealing Local Laws 29
>   Petitions 30
>   Where the Initiative and Referendum Work Best ... 30
>   Chapter 2 Review 30

Chapter 3: Similarities on the Local Level

>   Local Government Structure 35
>   Governing Body 35
>   Executive Branch 37
>   The Third Branch 37
>   Elections 38
>   Primary Elections 38
>   General Elections 38
>   Special Elections 38
>   Partisan and Nonpartisan 39
>   Eligibility to Vote 40
>   Your Vote Counts 40
>   Voter-Controlled Taxes 40
>   Property Tax 41
>   Income Tax 42
>   Sales Tax 43
>   A Word of Caution 44
>   Public Records and Open Meetings 44
>   Public Records 45
>   Open Meetings 46
>   Executive Sessions 46
>   Land Use and Development 47
>   Zoning 48
>   Planning 49

Contents   xi

        Subdivision Regulations 51
        Building Regulations 52
    Chapter 3 Review 53

Chapter 4: Managing in the Wilderness

    The Surveyed Township 59
        Land Grants 59
        Thomas Hutchins 61
        The Land Ordinance of 1785 63
    The Civil Township 65
        Original Responsibilities 65
    The Impact of Technology 66
        Changes in Transportation 67
        Changes in Communication 68
        The Declining Popularity of Civil Townships 68
    Chapter 4 Review 69

Chapter 5: Township Government Today

    Introduction 73
        Census Data 73
    The Dual Role of Township Trustees 76
        Township Clerk 76
    The Expanding Scope of Activities 76
        Original Tasks 77
        Increased Capabilities 78
        Special Districts 78
    Who Is In Charge Here? 79
    Limited Self-Government (1991) 80
    Limited Home Rule (1999) 81
    Township Boundaries 84
        Paper Townships 85
        Consolidation 86
        Further Obligations of County Commissions 87
    Township-Municipal Merger 88
    Chapter 5 Review 91

Chapter 6: County Government

Introduction 95
The Northwest Ordinance of 1787 96
    Government Structure of the Northwest Territory .. 96
    Creation of the Northwest Ordinance 96
Arthur St. Clair 97
    St. Clair's Early Life 97
    St. Clair's Accomplishments in America 98
    A Turbulent Tenure as Governor 99
    St. Clair Opposes Ohio Statehood 100
The First Counties 101
County Government Structure 104
    An Executive Branch with Many Twigs 104
    The Elected County Officials 104
    Sheriff 105
    Coroner 105
    Clerk of Courts 105
    Prosecuting Attorney 106
    Recorder 106
    Surveyor/Engineer 106
    Auditor and Treasurer 107
    Board of County Commissioners 107
    Term of Office and Salary 110
    The Judicial Branch 110
Chapter 6 Review 112

Chapter 7: County Home Rule

The Cincinnati Reform Movement 115
    Cincinnati's Boss Cox 116
    On to the County! 118
Charter Commissions 120
Charters By Petition 121
    The Summit County Charter 123
Opposition to Change 123
    Patronage 124
    The Grass Roots Connection 124
    Four Hurdles 124

Contents   xiii

    The Cuyahoga County Experience 125
        What is a Municipal Power? 126
        Cuyahoga County Today 126
    Alternative Forms of Government 127
        County Administrators 128
    Developments Elsewhere 128
    Chapter 7 Review 130

Chapter 8: The Municipal Life Cycle

    Introduction 135
    Incorporation 135
        Incorporation of a Village 136
        Incorporation of a City 137
        Frequency of Incorporation 139
        Incorporation of All or Most of a Township 139
        Quasi-Corporations 141
    Annexation 141
        Annexation of Unincorporated Land 141
        The Procedure Followed by Landowners 142
        Recent Annexations 142
        Transfer of Land Between Municipalities 144
    Merger 145
        Municipal to Municipal Merger 145
    Detachment 146
    Calling It Quits: Dissolving a Municipality 146
    Chapter 8 Review 148
    Appendix A: An Act to Incorporate the Town of
        Jeffersonville in the County of Fayette 151
    Appendix B: The Annexation War of the Year 2000 .. 157

Chapter 9: Ohio Municipal Government

    Introduction 163
    The Municipal Chief Executive Officer 164
        Mayor 164
        Manager 165
        Commission 166

Richard S. Childs and Council-Manager Government . 167
    The Childs Model 169
    Selling the Plan 170
Ohio Statutory and Optional Forms of Government ... 171
    General Statutory 172
    Optional Statutory 172
    Charter Government 173
    Administrator or Director of Administration. 173
Other Executive Offices 174
    Who's Who in City Hall 174
    Who's Who in Village Hall 175
The Legislative Branch 177
    Non-Charter Village Council 177
    Non-Charter City Council 177
    Alternative 1: The Method Established
      by State Statute 177
    Alternative 2: The Other Method 178
    Charter Councils 178
Mayor's Court 178
Chapter 9 Review 181
Appendix A: Statement of the Dayton Charter
  Commission 1913 185

Chapter 10: Public Schools

The Early Years 191
    Subscription Schools 191
The First Hundred Years, 1803–1903 192
Fate of the School Lands Program 192
    Building a Public School System 193
    Centralization Versus Decentralization 194
    High Schools 195
Samuel Lewis 195
One-Room School Houses 197
Consolidation 199
Public Schools Today 199
    State Board of Education 200
    School Districts 200

Contents

       Boundary Changes for Efficiency 201
       Inter-District Agreements 202
  School Boards 204
       County Boards of Education/County Educational
       Service Centers 204
       City Boards of Education 205
       Exempted Village Boards of Education 205
       Local Boards of Education 205
       Joint Vocational School Districts 205
  Elections Below the State Level 206
  School Management Staff 207
       Superintendent of Schools 207
       Business Manager 207
       Treasurer 207
  The Cleveland Experiment 208
  Paying for Ohio's Schools 209
  Chapter 10 Review 210

Epilogue 215

Appendix: All About Ohio 219

Glossary 223

Index 231

Acknowledgments 243

Photo and Illustration Credits 244

Chapter 1: THE THREE LEVELS OF GOVERNMENT

Introduction

There are three levels of government in the United States: federal, state, and local. Each is a part of our whole system of government and each depends on the others. To understand government in the United States, one must know about all three levels.

Federal Government and State Government

The "disunited states" of America became the United States of America when the proposed Constitution was ratified (1788) and implemented (1789). The Constitution became the supreme law of the land. As protector of the Union, the new federal government ascended to a level above that of the states. Until then, the 13 original states had been able to look down on the central government because they had more authority to govern than it did.

As the jurisdiction of the federal government extended westward, additional states were established, thus allowing government to follow citizens into the great wilderness territories. The establishment of additional states was not only in compliance with Congressional plans for westward expansion, but it was also necessary because 18th and early 19th century technology was woefully inadequate by today's standards. People communicated by voice or pen, and they traveled by horse or boat.

Just as the federal government found it necessary to divide huge land areas into states, the states found it necessary, in order to deliver services to the people, to divide themselves into smaller areas. Those smaller areas are the ancestors of today's local governments. They formed the third level of government.

1

Local Government

Currently, that third level of government in Ohio includes 88 *counties*, roughly 239 *cities*, 702 *villages*, 1,309 *townships*, and 611 *public school districts* (not counting 61 county or multi-county educational service centers and 49 joint vocational school districts). The number of counties remains constant, but the number of cities, villages, civil townships and public school districts change from time to time. The Ohio Constitution requires those five kinds of local government, each of which has the ability to perform specific functions. What is written in the Constitution is brief. In effect, the General Assembly is directed to provide by law for counties and civil townships (Article X) and for a public school system (Article VI). Municipal government is recognized, classified into cities and villages, and granted home rule powers (Article XVIII). The General Assembly, which is the legislative branch of the state government, has the ability to provide by law for additional kinds of local government. Those additional kinds of local governments are called *special purpose districts* which include, among many other things, regional airport authorities, regional transit authorities (ground, air, and water transportation), and port authorities (import-export facilities).

Local governments often overlap. Your home is located in a county and in a school district. It is also located in a city or village or a township. As a matter of fact, it might be located in a city or a village *and* a township. Overlapping does not create problems except where townships are involved (see Chapter 5).

The Impact of Local Government

While federal and state governments perform many necessary services, only relatively few of these services have a direct impact on the daily lives of individuals. On the other hand, most of the things that local governments do have a direct, continuing impact on individuals. Of all the levels, governments on the local level are the most directly responsible for public health, safety, and well-being. The quality of life in every community is determined to a great extent by the ability of its local governments to provide adequate services. Local government responsibilities include education, elections, emergency ambulance service, land use control, local streets and highways, traffic control, parks and recreation, police and fire protection, building safety, water supply and wastewater disposal, and the collection and disposal of trash and garbage. The list goes on, but the services mentioned above help demonstrate the close relationship between local government and the people.

Early Local Governments

Local governments were probably not even discussed during the Constitutional Convention. This is because local government was then, and still is, a part of state government. Local governments are sometimes called "creatures of the state" because the state creates them. Besides, local governments in what is now the United States did not amount to much when the Constitution was drafted. In that year, there were 13 states with a combined population of just over three million people. Most of them lived on farms. It took a week to travel 220 miles by stagecoach from Boston to New York City. (That is like taking a week to travel from Cincinnati to Cleveland!) Boston was then about the size that Delaware, Ohio is today (population 21,857). New York City was then about the size that Lancaster, Ohio is today (population 35,808).

Local governments did not become a significant factor in national affairs until the last half of the 20th century. Rapid growth in urban areas and resulting problems during the years following World War II attracted ever-increasing attention from the federal level. For example, on August 31, 1965, the federal Department of Housing and Urban Development (HUD) was established. HUD is a cabinet-level department created to deal with urban problems: it administers many federal grant-in-aid programs which are intended to improve the urban environment. A close relationship, sometimes friendly and sometimes stormy, has developed between local officials and HUD. The creation of HUD did not change the nature of local government. It did, however, recognize that the local level is an important part of our whole system of government.

Federalism

Federal, state and local governments interact. What one does affects the others. Questions concerning what those relationships *are* or what they *should be* have been debated in this country for over 200 years. What powers should each kind of government have? Should one be superior to the others? How many kinds of government do we need?

Federalism is a system of government in which power is divided by a written constitution between a central government and lower levels of government. It is the belief that powers can and should be divided between the national and state governments. With governmental powers divided, those who wrote the U.S. Constitution believed, the national government would never be strong enough to become oppressive even if it wanted to.

Federalism has become a field of study which deals with the division of power and the relationships between the federal government and the lower levels of government — both state and local. Today's relationships are quite different from those originally established by the U.S. Constitution. Major changes have taken place. If time travel were possible and if those who wrote the Constitution visited us today, they might believe that a second American Revolution had taken place.

The "Second American Revolution"

A successful revolution brings about major change. The first American Revolution (1775-1783) resulted in our independence from Great Britain. The second American Revolution is not as well known as the first. In fact, many Americans know little or nothing about it. The second American Revolution, although perhaps not yet concluded, has handed the federal government ever increasing authority over state and local governments. The second revolution started before the U.S. Constitution was ratified by the states and it has been going on ever since. Combatants include voters, politicians, teachers, public officials, judges and others. The issue? Federalism. During the last 50 years or so, the federal government has won most of the federalism battles.

The Intended Relationship

The proper balance between the states and the proposed central government was an emotional issue debated by the framers of the U.S. Constitution during the long, hot summer of 1787. Perhaps the most extreme action was taken by Luther Martin, delegate from Maryland. He quit the convention and returned home to give warning of what he believed to be a conspiracy to bring about total abolition and destruction of all state governments.

Figure 1-1: James Madison

When the work of the convention was finished, three delegates who favored ratification by the states, Alexander Hamilton, John Jay, and James Madison wrote a series of essays explaining the proposed Constitution. The essays were published under the heading, *The Federalist*. In *Federalist Number 45*, James Madison, often called the father of the Constitution, provided a concise statement of his understanding of the appropriate division of governing authority between the nation and the states under the federal system created by the Constitution. He wrote:

> The powers delegated by the proposed Constitution to the federal government are few and defined. Those which are to remain with the State Governments are numerous and indefinite. The former will be exercised principally on external objects, such as war, peace, negotiation, and foreign commerce, with which last the power of taxation will, for the most part, be connected. All the powers reserved to the several states will extend to all objects which, in the ordinary course of affairs, concern the lives, liberties, and properties of the people, and the internal order, improvement, and property of the State.

Basically, the new federal government was intended to do the things that the states could not do as well for themselves. Dealing with foreign countries, issuing and setting the value of money, and regulating trade are a few examples. These are *international* and *interstate* powers. The state governments believed themselves to be perfectly capable of taking care of things inside their own borders.

The Constitution provides for federalism by dividing powers between the federal and state governments. It does this primarily by stating and implying what the national government *can* do. What we call the *enumerated powers* are listed in Article I, Section 8. This section authorizes Congress to lay and collect taxes, issue and borrow money, regulate commerce, declare war, and so on. The constitutional division of powers was made even more permanent, or so it was thought, by adoption of the Bill of Rights in 1791.

The Bill of Rights
The proposed constitution had critics, and the so-called states rights advocates were among the most vocal. Some critics began calling for a second constitutional convention to correct what they viewed

The Three Levels of Government 7

as mistakes, even before the product of the first was ratified. The underlying theme of most criticism was fear that the new central government was given too much authority. Such criticism placed ratification in jeopardy.

Madison and his fellow federalists devised an inspired strategy to blunt criticism. They promised that the first task of the first Congress would be to propose "rights" amendments to the Constitution. The Constitution was ratified and Congress did, on September 25, 1789, approve a dozen amendments. The ten that were subsequently adopted are collectively known as the Bill of Rights (see below).

✓ Did you know?

In 1789, Congress submitted a dozen amendments for ratification or approval by the states. Two of these amendments were not ratified. Those not ratified dealt with: (1) compensation to members of Congress, and (2) the ratio of members in the House of Representatives to population.

The ten amendments that *were* ratified are known as the **Bill of Rights**. The subject headings of the these first ten amendments of the Constitution are listed below:

Amendment 1	Freedom of Religion, Speech and the Press; Right of Assembly
Amendment 2	Right to Keep and Bear Arms
Amendment 3	Quartering of Troops
Amendment 4	Limiting the Right of Search
Amendment 5	Guaranty of Trial by Jury; Private Property to Be Protected
Amendment 6	Rights of Accused Persons
Amendment 7	Rules of Common Law
Amendment 8	Excessive Bail, Fines, and Punishment Prohibited
Amendment 9	Rights Retained by the People
Amendment 10	Powers Reserved to States and People

The Tenth Amendment is known as the States Rights Amendment. It provides that:

> The powers not delegated to the United States by the Constitution, nor prohibited by it to the states, are reserved to the States respectively or to the people.

The Federal-State Relationship Today

The relationship between federal and state government is quite different today than it was 200 years ago. At first, each was in charge of its own affairs. The current relationship is vertical with the federal government clearly at the top. No longer is the federal government limited to handling international and interstate affairs. Today, state borders are no obstacle to federal authority and the federal government is deeply involved in what used to be considered internal state (intrastate) affairs. Writing in 1985, U.S. Supreme Court Justice Sandra Day O'Connor observed that:

> The central issue of federalism . . . is whether any area remains in which a state may act free of federal interference. *Garcia v. San Antonio Transit Authority.*

How did the federal government gain such power over state and local government? The answer can be found in the decisions of the U.S. Supreme Court. No single decision declared the federal government supreme. Instead, power was gained one case at a time. The U.S. Constitution, as interpreted by the Supreme Court, is the supreme law of the land. As time goes by, our society changes. Supreme Court justices retire and are replaced. Changed conditions can invoke new interpretations of the Constitution. What was once prohibited, the court decides, is now allowed.

The Commerce Clause Versus the Tenth Amendment

Many federalism battles (court cases) have pitted the Commerce Clause against the Tenth Amendment. Article 1, Section 8c of the

U.S. Constitution gives Congress the power "to regulate commerce with foreign nations, and among the several states, and with the Indian tribes." *Commerce* is defined by a standard dictionary as "the exchange of goods, products, or property, as between states or nations." It would seem reasonable to conclude that the Commerce Clause applies to *interstate* commerce only. After all, the Constitution uses the specific words "*among* the several states." This is not the case, however. Lawyers have argued and the courts have agreed that anything having a direct or indirect effect on interstate commerce is subject to regulation by Congress. Thus, the Commerce Clause has been a source of vast federal power with dire consequences for state and local governments.

Writing in 1935, Chief Justice Charles Evans Hughes observed:

> If the commerce clause were construed to reach all enterprises and transactions which could be said to have an indirect effect on interstate commerce, the federal authority would embrace practically all of the activities of the people, and the authority of the state over its domestic concerns would exist only by the sufferance of the federal government.

His observation was a prophecy which was vividly illustrated 50 years later in a Supreme Court case known as *Garcia v. San Antonio Metropolitan Transit Authority (469 U.S. 528, 1985).* The Garcia case was the biggest federalism victory ever for the national government!

The Garcia Case

Garcia was an employee of local government. He worked for the transit authority, which operates in and around San Antonio, Texas. The question before the court was whether the transit authority must abide by the federal Fair Labor Standards Act (FLSA). The Act, among other things, regulates hours of work and overtime pay. Predictably, lawyers for the federal government used the Commerce Clause to justify federal regulation and lawyers for the local government used the Tenth Amendment to oppose federal regulation. The court found in favor of the federal government for several reasons:

- The transit authority received federal money;
- Transit systems owned by governments are not much different than those privately owned;
- Transit employees, both public and private, who cross state lines are subject to the Fair Labor Standards Act;
- The court rejected a distinction between "traditional" and "non-traditional" municipal activities — a distinction which was formerly accepted.

It was determined that local governments are subject to the federal wage and hour requirements. The consequence of the decision is that if one municipal activity is subject to FLSA, all municipal activities are subject to FLSA.

As a part of the *Garcia* decision, the court issued an astonishing announcement. It gave notice that it will no longer referee commerce power disputes between the Congress and the lower levels of government. After years and years of litigation, the Tenth Amendment has been weakened to the extent that it is no longer a restraint on the power of Congress to regulate commerce. Commerce power disputes, the court decreed, are henceforth political issues, not constitutional issues. If the lower levels of government have a commerce power problem, they can lobby Congress for a political remedy just as any special interest group does.

The significance of *Garcia* is not that the governments on the lower levels lost another Supreme Court case. The significance is the crushing magnitude of that defeat. A major change in our federal system took place in 1985 and the general public hardly noticed.

Recent Commerce Clause Decisions

Since *Garcia*, Congress has sought the outer limits of its new-found authority. Recent attempts to utilize the fruits of the *Garcia* decision have triggered judicial resistance. Congressional overreaching has not allowed the Supreme Court to abdicate its role as referee.

Statutes supposedly based on commerce powers have been struck down. In 1992, the Supreme Court invalidated a law which made it a federal offense to possess a gun near a school. The court found that bearing arms is in no sense an economic activity that substantially affects interstate commerce (*United States vs. Lopez*). In 2000, the court struck down portions of the Violence Against Women Act. That Act made "gender-motivated" violence against women (such as battering and/or rape) a federal crime which could be tried in a federal court. The Supreme Court ruled that "gender-motivated" violence is not an economic activity.

Why did Congress use the Commerce Clause to justify federal control over those two matters? Because it was thought to be a way to bypass state jurisdiction.

Federalization

Increasingly, state and local governments are becoming the servants of the federal government. The trend in this direction has been called the "federalization" or the "nationalization" of those lower level governments. Whether it is a necessary and desirable trend should be decided by an informed citizenry. The balance struck 200 years ago was not by unanimous consent. Federalism is a changing concept influenced by economic, social, and political conditions. Since change does occur, it is incumbent on the people to be aware of the changes and to guide the direction of change.

The Exercise of Federal Power

If the federal government is the level furthest removed from the people, how can it enforce its will throughout the land? The federal government reaches down to where the people are by using state and local governments to enforce its laws. It does this with (1) payments through grant-in-aid programs, (2) assurances from grant-in-aid recipients, (3) partial preemptions of authority, and (4) direct orders.

Payments

Payments by the federal government to lower level governments are called *grants-in-aid*. The number of federal grant-in-aid programs offered to state and local governments changes each year. The Year 2000 Catalog of Federal Domestic Assistance (catalog of federal grant programs) lists 1,425 programs administered by 57 federal agencies. Annual grant awards (payments) amount to approximately $300 billion. Of those totals, roughly one-half of the programs and two-thirds of the money is intended for state and local governments. This money is not given to state and local governments to spend as they see fit; it is given to carry out federal programs. Payments are made to those whose applications to operate one or more of the programs are accepted and approved. Some grants are awarded by the federal government directly to local governments. Other federal grant programs operated by local governments are supervised by state government. Programs and funding not intended for state and local government are available to individuals, non-profit corporations, U.S. territories, and native American tribal governments.

Grant-in-aid categories are: Agriculture, Business and Commerce, Community Development, Consumer Protection, Cultural Affairs, Disaster Prevention and Relief, Education, Employment and Training, Energy, Environmental Quality, Food and Nutrition, Health, Housing, Income Security and Social Services, Information and Statistics, Law and Legal Services, Natural Resources, Regional Development, Science and Technology, and Transportation.

Assurances

Recipients of grant money are required to give promises or assurances that they will abide by and enforce federal laws and regulations which are applicable to the program being funded. The resulting list of laws and regulations can fill several typed pages. This practice greatly increases federal enforcement capabilities: every grantee becomes an enforcement agent!

Partial Preemptions

Grants-in-aid are only one way to get things done. Sometimes the U.S. Congress will decide to let state governments do something if the state government will do it the way Congress wants it done. This type of provision in a federal law is referred to as a *partial preemption*. Under partial preemption, the federal government retains control of a program, but is willing to delegate operational responsibilities to state or local governments. The willingness lasts only as long as the state or local government follows the federal standards or guidelines. As long as those guidelines are followed, the federal government provides funds. Ohio's Unemployment Compensation System, which is operated by a state agency to help people who lose their jobs, is an example of a partial preemption. Federal standards cover such items as who is eligible for unemployment benefits, how the amount of benefit is calculated, how long the benefits will be paid, and how disputes over benefits are settled. Among the more recent partial preemptions are laws affecting the environment (with the major players being federal and state environmental protection agencies).

Figure 1-2: Cartoon Depiction of Environmental Partial Preemption by the Federal Government

Reprinted, with permission, from the Columbus Dispatch.

Direct Orders
So far, we have discussed three methods by which the federal government can reach down to the people. Those three methods all involve cooperation. A fourth method is available which involves no cooperation at all. The federal government can simply order the lower level governments to comply with a federal law. Direct orders which are resisted become the issues over which the federalism battles are fought. They become the cases appealed to the U.S. Supreme Court. For example, the *Garcia* case started with an order from the Wage and Hour Division of the U.S. Department of Labor directing the San Antonio Transit Authority to comply with the Fair Labor Standards Act. The local officials refused. Consequently, the court action began.

Total Preemptions and Mandates
Some direct-order laws and regulations *prohibit* certain state or local government actions. For example, state and local governments cannot regulate something that the federal government has deregulated and vice versa. Those kinds of federal laws and regulations which reserve certain matters for the federal government are known as *total preemptions*. The regulation of radio and television signals, for example, is the province of federal authority only. On the other hand, some federal orders *require* state or local government actions. Federal laws that require local action are known as *mandates*. Federally-imposed mandates have become a major federalism issue. Political philosophy aside, unfunded mandates impose major financial burdens which state and local government officials find highly objectionable.

Federal and state legislators are showing some empathy for the plight of local government officials. The 1995 "Unfunded Mandates Reform Act" provides that a roll call vote can be instigated by any member of Congress when an unfunded mandate is being considered. From a political point of view, the members of Congress are placed in an awkward position if they vote for the mandate without providing adequate funding. The people back home might demand explanations. The Ohio General Assembly has in a *very* small way recognized the problem. Twice during the 123rd

Session (1999-2000), bills were introduced to lessen the impact of state-imposed unfunded mandates on local governments. One bill was reported out of committee but no action was taken by either the House or the Senate. The second bill died in committee.

Chapter 1 Review

■ Summary

Government in the United States exists on three levels: national, state, and local. Governments on each level possess a degree of sovereignty (freedom from external control). The relationships among the three levels define and constitute an overall system of government entitled *federalism*.

The federalism established by the founding fathers has changed significantly, especially since the 1930s. The jurisdiction of the national government has expanded while state jurisdiction has diminished. Change has been facilitated by numerous decisions of the U.S. Supreme Court. Most cases involving state or local governments have been decided in favor of the federal government.

Perhaps the most significant of all the federalism cases was *Garcia v. San Antonio Metropolitan Transit Authority (1985)*. It confirmed that the Commerce Clause is more powerful than the Constitution's Tenth Amendment. Even though the Supreme Court, after *Garcia*, decided to leave commerce power questions to the political process, the attempted overreaching by Congress has kept the Court in its referee role.

Today, the federal government uses state and local governments to enforce its laws. It does this with (1) payments through grant-in-aid programs, (2) assurances from grant-in-aid recipients, (3) partial preemptions, and (4) direct orders. Those direct orders that require local action are called *mandates*, while those that prohibit local action are called *preemptions*.

■ Glossary

Bill of Rights. The first ten amendments to the U.S. Constitution. Amendments are restrictions on the federal government.

Commerce. The production, transportation, buying and selling of goods and services.

Community. A group of people in a defined area living under common laws and rules.

Constitution. A statement of functions and fundamental principles according to which a nation or state is governed. The supreme law of the land.

Federal. Pertaining to a form of government in which states have relinquished some sovereignty in order to form a union of states and a central (usually called federal) government. In this definition, **sovereignty** means freedom from external control.

Federalism. A system of government wherein powers are divided between a central government and other (lower) levels of government. Each government is supreme within its sphere of authority. The opposite of a "unitary" system of government wherein the central government is supreme in all matters.

Government. The authority to control the affairs of people living in a community.

Grant-in-Aid. A grant, usually a sum of money, by a central government to a lower level government to carry out a policy or program.

Municipal. Pertaining to a city or village.

Public. The people as a whole; all of the people.

The Three Levels of Government 17

Revolution. A complete overthrow of an established government.

State. A sovereign political community with a distinct government which is (1) recognized as supreme by the people, and (2) has jurisdiction over a given territory. In this definition, **political** pertains to government or public, as opposed to private.

States Rights Amendment. The Tenth Amendment to the U.S. Constitution. A part of the Bill of Rights. The basic principle of U.S. federalism is fixed in the Tenth Amendment which provides that the national government is to exercise only those powers delegated to it with all other powers reserved to the states or people.

■ **Review Questions**
1. Name the three levels of government in the United States. *Fed, State, Local*
2. Municipal governments are found on which level? *Local*
3. Governments on what level are most directly responsible for public health, safety, and well being? ~~State~~ *Local*
4. Why are local governments often called "creatures of the state?" *created by the state*
5. Federalism deals with the division of ___*Powers*___ among the three levels of government.
6. Which amendment to the U.S. Constitution relates directly to federalism? *10*
7. Did James Madison envision strong or weak state governments? *Strong*
8. In an interstate commerce case involving a city before the U.S. Supreme Court, city lawyer "A" bases his arguments on the Tenth Amendment while the opposition lawyer "B" bases her arguments on the Commerce Clause. Who is most likely to win? *B*
9. Payments made by the federal government to state or local governments to carry out federal policies or programs are called ___*Grant-in-aid*___.
10. Orders by the federal government to carry out federal policies or programs without payment by the federal government are *unfunded mandates*

called _____.

Answers to Review Questions: 1. National (or federal), state and local; 2. Third (local) level; 3. Third (local) level; 4. They are created by the state; 5. Powers; 6. Tenth; 7. Strong; 8. Lawyer "B"; 9. Grants-in-Aid; 10. Unfunded mandates.

Chapter 2: DIFFERENCES ON THE LOCAL LEVEL

When purchasing a home, some buyers give little attention to whether it is located inside or outside a municipality. They ask about services such as police, fire, and trash collection. When assured that services are available, it is easy to conclude that it makes no difference whether the house is located inside or outside a city or village.

House hunters tend to ask about things that are tangible. They can see the police patrol cars, fire trucks, and trash compactors. There are, however, differences among local governments which cannot be seen. Knowledge of those differences can be a major factor in the house hunter's decision. Those intangible but nevertheless real differences include: (1) the ability of the local government to practice self-government, and (2) the ability of citizens to participate in that self-government. Some of the more significant facets of self-government are home rule, charter government, and direct democracy (the initiative and referendum).

Origin

Counties and Townships

Counties and townships were created first by the territorial government and later by the state government to perform tasks assigned by those governments. They are a part of the overall pattern of government (state, county, township) created for the Northwest Territory by the Continental Congress.

Counties and townships were created without regard to local wishes. The people did not ask for those local governments. Counties and townships were mandated in what is now Ohio by a federal law known as the Ordinance of 1787. That law is also known as the Northwest Ordinance because it contains instructions and plans for extending government to the lands northwest of the Ohio River. Those lands became what are now the states of Ohio (1803), Indiana (1816), Illinois (1818), Michigan (1837), Wisconsin (1848), and Minnesota (1858).

Figure 2-1: The Land Area of Northwest Territory

Northwest Territory

The Ordinance of 1787 created a temporary (territorial) government for the Northwest Territory to function until states were formed. The chief executive was the governor, appointed by the Continental Congress. He was instructed by section eight of the Ordinance to "proceed, from time to time, to lay out parts of the district in which the Indian titles shall have been extinguished, into counties and townships . . . ." The Ordinance refers to the whole Northwest Territory as "the district." Nine counties were created in what is

Differences on the Local Level 21

now Ohio before Ohio achieved statehood. Washington County, formed in 1788, was the first. It follows then that the first townships were formed in Washington County.

Safety and justice for the settlers required organized government throughout the Northwest Territory (thus, the need for states, counties, and townships). The creation of Washington County was the second law enacted by the temporary government of the Northwest Territory. The first law established a militia. Other early laws established a court system and the office of sheriff.

Municipal government is not mentioned in the Northwest Ordinance. It is of interest to note, however, that legislative actions taken by the temporary government *did* say where the action was taken. Here are the concluding words written into the law establishing the office of sheriff:

> Published in the City of Marietta, County of Washington, Territory of the United States, N.W. of the Ohio River, and upon this 23rd day of August, in the thirteenth year of the sovereignty and independence of the United States, and of our LORD one thousand, seven hundred and eighty-eight.

It appears that Marietta was cited as a city not because it possessed any legal stature but, instead, simply because it was there. It was the first permanent settlement in the Northwest Territory. Years later, speaking during a Fourth of July ceremony in 1876, Dr. Israel Ward Andrews of Marietta College set the record straight. He said:

> As Washington was the first county established in the Northwest Territory, so Marietta was the first town incorporated. As a township it was established by the Court of Quarter Session in 1790. As a town it was established by the territorial legislature on December 2, 1800. The town of Athens was incorporated December 6 of the same year, Cincinnati January 1st, 1802, and Chillicothe, January 4, 1802.

The dates given by Dr. Andrews do not correspond to those listed today by the Ohio Secretary of State's Office. Why? Because those places were incorporated again, this time by the Ohio General Assembly, after statehood was achieved. The Court of Quarter Session, mentioned by Dr. Andrews, had many powers now exercised by county commissions. As each county was established, members for its Court of Quarter Session were appointed by the Governor. They met quarterly to attend to the business of the county government. The work of the Territorial Government was not lost when Ohio attained statehood. Instead, those accomplishments served as a basis upon which to build.

Municipalities

Even without municipalities, every place in Ohio is covered by governments of one kind or another. A comprehensive structure consisting of township, county, state, and federal government extends from the local to the national levels. Why then, do we have municipal governments?

Throughout the ages, people have congregated for a variety of reasons: safety, commerce, education, and so on. The resulting communities are crowded with people and those people require many services not found (or not available at a sufficient level) in rural areas. Typical among those services would be adequate police and fire protection, a dependable fresh water supply, a wastewater disposal system, and conveniently located highways.

Citizens, not government, start the incorporation process by which municipal governments are formed. Municipal governments are created to provide for the special needs of people who live in urban places. Our house hunters, mentioned in the opening paragraphs of this chapter, would do well to consider the genealogy of the local government which will serve their future needs. The widest assortment of powers applicable to living conditions in urban places is available to municipal government.

Home Rule

Home rule means local self-government. To understand home rule, we must first make a distinction between "local government" and "local self-government."

Local government. All governments below the state level are local governments. This includes – but is not limited to – counties, municipalities, townships, and school districts.

Local self-government. Local self-government is the ability of a local government to control its own affairs by enacting and enforcing local laws. The powers of local self-government are known as home rule.

Notice how often the word "local" is used when explaining home rule. Local laws can deal with local issues only. They cannot deal with state-wide issues. Land zoning is an example of a strictly local issue. Child adoption criteria is an example of a state-wide issue. Municipal government is the only kind of local government which is created with home rule powers. In fact, the Ohio Constitution guarantees that Ohio cities and villages can practice local self-government from the moment they are created.

Counties and townships were not created with home rule powers, but they can acquire some. They earn the right to practice limited home rule by changing their government. Residents must vote to approve the change. As of January 1, 2001, only one county and 14 townships had earned the right to practice limited self-government.

Without home rule, state statues control every aspect of a local government. State law specifies how the local government is organized and how it must operate. State law tells the local government what it can control and how to do it. It is usually very difficult to obtain changes in the state law because every change affects many local governments. Home rule allows a local government to conduct its own internal affairs without the constraints of state law.

Cities and villages have home rule. Counties and townships can have limited home rule. Other kinds of local government, including school districts and some other special purpose districts, cannot obtain even limited home rule. Neither the state constitution nor state laws provide a way for it to happen. When a person stops to think about it, what kind of laws would they pass anyway?

Municipal Home Rule
Since 1912, the Ohio Constitution has stated:

> Municipalities shall have authority to exercise all powers of local self-government and to adopt and enforce within their limits such . . . regulations as are not in conflict with general laws.

(Article 18, Sec. 3)

General laws are state laws which apply state-wide to matters which must be regulated and controlled uniformly throughout the state. Any list of such matters would include, for example, marriage and adoption laws, the control of major crimes, and the regulation of the court system.

Municipal Laws: Ordinances
Municipal laws are called *ordinances*. Cities and villages have passed ordinances on hundreds of subjects. Typical ordinances deal with such matters as:

- Administrative code (responsibilities and duties of the municipality's management officials);
- Animals (loose, nuisance, and vicious);
- Buildings (construction, demolition, and safety);
- Business regulations (licenses and permits);
- Development (subdivision and urban renewal);
- Motor vehicles (noise, equipment, and safety);
- Nuisances (such as trash, weeds, and loud radios);
- Refuse (trash and garbage collection and disposal);
- Sewage (collection and disposal);
- Traffic (truck routes, school zones, and parking);
- Water (storm and drinking);
- Zoning (land use).

So many ordinances accumulate over a period of years that many municipalities *codify* their ordinances. When ordinances are codified, those ordinances of a permanent and lasting nature are put into book form. This is a real convenience for both municipal officials and the public. The book of codified ordinances is referred to as the city or village code.

While inside a municipality, people are subject to not only federal and state laws but also to municipal law. The likelihood of conflict among laws passed by those governments is small. A great deal of legal precedent has accumulated over the years. However, in the event a conflict does arise and cannot be settled amiably, the dispute can be resolved like any other — in court.

Township Home Rule
Some ability to control their own affairs was given to townships in 1991 and more was given in 1999.

The 1991 enactment granted what the General Assembly chose to call *Limited Self-government*. It conferred, among other things, a limited ability to legislate. Township laws are called *resolutions*. Although the scope of legislation was limited to misdemeanors (minor offenses) and fines, the ability to legislate was a major change to township government in Ohio.

The state legislators decided to use the term *Limited Home Rule* instead of *Limited Self-government* in 1999 legislation, a change which contributed nothing but confusion. The new status (home rule) was granted to those with the old status (self-government). Among other things, the 1999 legislation increased townships' ability to regulate construction by private contractors and/or to carry out their own construction projects.

Voter approval must be obtained before home rule powers can be exercised. (See Chapter 5 for more information concerning township home rule.)

County Home Rule
The Ohio Constitution offers limited self-government to counties. Counties can enact local laws if they make changes to their government. They can either (1) adopt an alternative form of

government, or (2) adopt a charter (both of which are explained in Chapter 7). However, the gift of county home rule has limited lawmaking value. Except under special circumstances which have never been met, county laws cannot supersede municipal ordinances or township regulations. A "special circumstance" might be the transfer of certain township and municipal responsibilities to the county government. Voters might, for example, approve a county charter which gives the county exclusive responsibility for a countywide water supply and distribution system. In such an event, county statutes in regard to water supply and distribution would control county-wide.

No county has adopted an alternative form of government. Only Summit County has adopted a charter and it assumes no township or municipal functions.

✓ Did you know?

In Ohio, *all* municipalities have the ability to practice home rule. This is not the case with counties or townships. Percentages of local governments with the ability to practice home rule (as of 2000) are:

Municipalities	100%
Counties	A little over 1%
Townships	A little over 1%

Charters

When approved by the voters, a *charter* is like a constitution. It defines how the government is organized, how its powers are distributed, and how the government operates. In other words, a charter tells how the government is put together and how it works. Adoption of a charter is a two-step process. First, voters establish a charter commission and elect 15 members. The commission has up to one year to draft a proposed charter and to make the contents known to the community. The question of adoption then appears on the ballot for approval or rejection.

Municipal Charters

By 2001, there were 238 charter municipalities in Ohio. This includes 182 cities and 56 villages with populations ranging from over 650,000 (City of Columbus) to about 500 (Village of Glenwillow). The first Ohio municipal charters were adopted in 1913 by the cities of Cleveland, Dayton, Lakewood, Middletown, and Springfield. Some of the things that municipal voters can do with a charter are:

- Specify the number and duties of elected officials;
- Decide whether the chief executive will be appointed or elected;
- Create operating departments (such as police, fire, etc.) and management positions;
- Establish special rules which must be followed by the municipal government. The rules can deal with such things as personnel, taxes, and the way ordinances are enacted.

A well prepared charter creates a custom-made government that fits a particular community. A city or village without a charter follows state law concerning how the municipal government *must* be organized and how it *must* operate. For example, the state law requires that specific departments be established and it specifies which offices must be filled by election and which by appointment. It establishes the chain of command. State law also establishes personnel and fiscal practices. These kinds of state requirements can be changed significantly by a charter adopted by a vote of the people.

State law mandates how non-charter cities and villages are organized and how they must operate. There are significant differences between city requirements and village requirements. Consequently, some villages, as their population grows near the point (5,000 residents) when they must become a city, adopt a charter. Thus, population growth does not dictate their form of government; instead their charter rules.

County Charters
Many attempts have been made to adopt county charters. Charter questions have been on the ballot of 11 Ohio counties; all but one failed. The only successful attempt to create and adopt a charter was made by Summit County. Summit County has won the right to practice limited home rule. County efforts to adopt charters are detailed in Chapter 7.

Direct Democracy
The Pledge of Allegiance states: "I pledge allegiance to the flag of the United States of America and to the *republic* for which it stands . . ." (emphasis added). Contrary to popular belief, our national government is not a democracy; it is a republic. In a true democracy, every citizen has a equal voice in the government. Every citizen can speak and vote on every law or issue being considered. In a true democracy, decisions are made by the people.

When the U.S. Constitution was being written, the population of the country was a little over three million people. Of that total, there were approximately one million adult males who were eligible to vote. The founding fathers who wrote the Constitution decided that very little would be accomplished if a million people voted on every proposed law. It would take months and months of counting after each vote! Instead of establishing a democracy, they established a republic. A republic is a *representative* democracy. In a republic, decisions are made by representatives of the people.

Local governments are small representative democracies, but it is possible for their citizens to participate directly in the legislative (law making) process if they desire to do so. Unlike government on the federal level, true "democracy" exists on the local level. Citizens themselves can enact or repeal laws. They can do so by using powers known as the *initiative* and *referendum*. Those powers are reserved to the people by the Ohio Constitution.

The Initiative and Referendum

Initiative simply means "to initiate" and referendum means "to refer." Using the initiative procedure, citizens can place the enactment of a new law or the repeal of an existing law on the ballot. By using the referendum procedure, citizens can refer a newly enacted law to the judgment of the people. Referendum delays the enforcement of a newly enacted law until it is approved by the voters. The new law dies if it is not approved by the voters. Laws initiated by the people are not always enacted, nor are laws referred to the people always repealed. Nevertheless, citizens have the opportunity to try! This opportunity does not exist at the federal level, but it does exist at the state level. However, any effort to enact or repeal a state law requires the well-organized help of a great many workers and a sizeable budget. The initiative and referendum work best on the local level.

Enacting and Repealing Local Laws

Who can enact a local law? Both the legislature of the local government and its citizens. Municipal governments can enact laws and so can their citizens by following the initiative procedure. The citizens of Akron, for example, can enact laws for the City of Akron.

Likewise, both the legislature of the local government and its citizens can repeal a newly-enacted law. Citizens can follow the referendum procedure. However, there are exceptions to the referendum rule. The major exception relates to local laws passed as emergency measures. When this is done, the law makers say, in effect, "We have an emergency on our hands and this law is necessary to deal with it quickly." Laws passed as emergency measures are not subject to referendum. Many lively arguments have erupted between law makers and their constituents over what is or is not an emergency situation. Sometimes a law deals with a perceived "emergency" which does not invoke, in those opposed to it, a sense of urgency. Take, for example, a requirement that smoke detectors be installed in all multiple dwellings (apartments). Members of council might believe that delay can cost lives. Owners of the apartment buildings might wish to leave the door open to referendum.

Petitions
A petition is used to start the initiative or the referendum procedure. State law spells out what the petition must say and how it is circulated. Only registered voters of the local jurisdiction involved can sign the petition. Only Akron citizens, for example, can sign a petition dealing with Akron law. State law sets the number of necessary signatures at ten percent of the number of votes cast within the local jurisdiction for governor when that office was last elected. Charters can provide a slightly different procedure. The number of signatures required might be increased or decreased.

City petitions are filed with the city auditor or city clerk. Village petitions are filed with the village clerk. Township petitions are filed with the township clerk. The charter of Summit County, the only county with a charter, provides that the petitions be filed with the clerk of the county council. State petitions are filed with the Secretary of State.

Where the Initiative and Referendum Work Best
The broad scope of municipal home rule offers by far the widest range of topics for legislation by the people. For that reason, the initiative and referendum are listed among the attributes which set municipal government apart from other local governments.

Chapter 2 Review

■ Summary

There are intangible but nevertheless real differences among local governments. Two differences featured in this chapter are: (1) the ability of the local government to practice self-government, and (2) the ability of citizens to participate in that self-government.

In 1787, the Continental Congress established a system of government for the Northwest Territory. That system called for the establishment of states, counties, and townships. The design created a network of governments reaching from the national to the local level. This arrangement mandated government for the wilderness lands. Municipal government was not mandated by the federal government, nor is it required by the state government. It is initiated by people to serve their communal needs.

Significant facets of self-government are home rule, charter government, and direct democracy: the initiative and referendum.

Home rule means local self-government. Local self-government is the ability of local government to control its own affairs by passing local laws. Municipal governments are created with home rule powers. Counties and townships can acquire limited home rule powers. By January 2000, one county and 14 townships had done so.

Charters are like constitutions. With a charter, the people can design and implement a custom-made local government. There are 238 charter municipalities in Ohio. Only one county, Summit County, has adopted a charter. State law tells local governments without charters how they must operate.

Citizens can initiate and repeal local laws. These rights, called the initiative and referendum, also allow citizens to control state law. However, such an effort on a state-wide basis takes many workers and a great deal of money. The initiative and referendum work best on the local level. The broad scope of municipal home rule offers by far the widest range of topics for legislation by the people.

■ Glossary

Charter. A document which defines how the government is organized, how its powers are distributed, and how the government operates. In other words, it tells how the government is put together and how it works. The charter is the basic law of the local government.

Charter Government. A government which operates according to a charter.

Constituency. The residents of a district represented by an elective officer.

Home Rule. Self-government in local matters by a local government.

Incorporation. The process by which the inhabitants of a community obtain legal status for that community and its people by forming a municipal corporation. The municipal corporation is an artificial person in the eyes of the law.

Initiative. The process by which the electorate initiates or enacts legislation. Issues are placed on the ballot by petition.

Legislative Process. The procedure followed by legislative bodies while enacting a law.

Petition. A formal written request.

Referendum. The submission of a recently enacted law to a vote of the people for ratification or rejection. The process is started by petition. In effect, voters can veto a law enacted by their legislature.

Republic. A representative democracy.

Self-government. Home rule for local affairs.

Special Purpose District. A local government established to provide a single service. Water and drainage, fire protection, and sanitary sewer districts are examples of special purpose districts. School districts are classified separately by the Bureau of Census.

■ Review Questions

1. Governmental organization in the Northwest Territory was established by what federal law?
2. Was municipal government included in the governmental organization mentioned in question (1)? Why do we have municipal governments?
3. What kind of local government has the widest array of powers to deal with living conditions in urban places?
4. (True or false) The terms, "home rule" and "self-government" mean the same thing.
5. What kind of local government always has home rule powers?
6. (True or false) Municipal laws are called ordinances.
7. (True or false) Most of the county and township governments in Ohio have acquired limited self-government.
8. By creating and adopting a _____, citizens can have a custom-made local government.
9. How many townships in Ohio have charters? How many counties?
10. Using the _____ and _____, people can enact and repeal legislation.

Answers to Review Questions: 1. The Ordinance of 1787; 2. No. To provide for the special needs of people who live in urban areas; 3. Municipal; 4. True; 5. Municipal; 6. True; 7. False; 8. Charter; 9. None. One; 10. Initiative and referendum.

Chapter 3: SIMILARITIES ON THE LOCAL LEVEL

In Chapter 2, we learned that there are intangible but real differences among local governments. The ability of the local government and its citizens to practice local self-government is the primary difference. There are also features and practices which are applicable to all local governments. Persons who move from one Ohio community to another can take heart! The new community may be alien, but in some ways its government will be familiar. While the diverse functions described in this chapter are not directly related to one another, they are all attributes of local government. Some of the things that local governments have in common include: structure, elections, public records and open meetings, voter-controlled taxes, and the ability to control land use and development.

Local Government Structure

All local governments have a governing body and an executive branch; some also have a judicial branch.

Governing Body

Persons elected to serve on the governing body make, within the parameters of state law, the major decisions concerning what the local government will do. They establish policy. Where there is self-government, the governing body is also a legislative body. Members of a legislative body enact laws. While duties differ somewhat depending on the type of local government involved, it is safe to assume that members of all governing bodies hear from constituents, manage finances, adopt plans and goals for the government, and monitor the work of the executive branch.

Members of governing bodies serve on a part-time basis. Most of them have full-time employment apart from their governmental duties. They participate in scheduled meetings and for their time and effort, they usually receive modest compensation. Time required and compensation received is generally in direct ratio to the population of the community served. Using municipal government as an example, a member of a small village council (1,000 population) will receive perhaps $800 per year while a member of a large city council (50,000 population) might receive $8,000 per year. The members of a few governing bodies receive no compensation at all! People become candidates for governing-body membership not for monetary reward, but instead for an opportunity to help make their home community a better place in which to live.

Governing bodies are known by the different names listed in Table 3-1 below.

Table 3-1: Names of Local Governing Bodies

Local Government	Name of Governing Body
County	Board of County Commissions
Township	Board of Township Trustees
City	City Council
Village	Village Council
School District	Board of Education

As we shall see in Chapter 6, the county commission has limited or no control over many county operations. However, the county commission is the closest thing there is to a governing body for county government. County commissions do have authority over their county's taxes, debt, and budget.

Similarities on the Local Level 37

Executive Branch
People in the executive branch do the daily work for which the government is responsible. Teachers, firefighters, trash collectors, and a host of others are all a part of one executive branch or another. The size of the executive branch depends on the population and size of the area to be served. Large county and city governments have thousands of employees in their executive branch. Small townships and villages have only a few employees. In response to one survey, 18 villages with populations between 950 and 1,050 reported that, on average, they employed three full-time and six part-time and/or seasonal employees. Ohio's largest city, Columbus, employed a work force of 8,328 full-time and 723 part-time and/or seasonal employees during the year 2000.

The people in charge of the executive branch are usually found in a special building as indicated in Table 3-2.

Table 3-2: Where to Find the People in Charge

Local Government	Name of Building
County	County Court House
Township	Township Hall
City	City Hall
Village	Village Hall
School District	School Administration Building

Other branches of the local government are usually found in the same building. One exception can be the township. Some communities do not have a township hall. The trustees might meet just about anywhere — perhaps in a fire station or some other place accessible to the public.

The Third Branch
On the sub-state level, only municipal and county governments have courts. Figure 6-5 in Chapter 6 shows the Ohio court system.

Municipal and county courts are a part of that formal, official structure. In addition, some cities and villages conduct what is known as Mayor's Court, which is a less formal proceeding as explained in Chapter 9.

Elections

Primary Elections

There are three kinds of elections: primary, general, and special. *Primary elections* are held during the month of May. Although the major purpose of a primary election is to select candidates, issues can also appear on the ballot. Candidates are people who seek to run for a public office such as mayor or county commissioner. An issue appears on the ballot as a question. For example, "Shall Ordinance Number 97-3, requiring smoke detectors in all multiple dwellings, be repealed?"

General Elections

General elections for federal, state, and county governments are held during even-numbered years (2002, 2004, and so on). General elections held during even-numbered years are also known as "regular state elections." General elections for local governments other than county are held in odd-numbered years (2001, 2003, and so on); they are also referred to as "regular municipal elections."

General elections are held during the month of November. This is when candidates win or lose their race for public office. Issues also appear on the November ballot.

Special Elections

Special elections can be held in February, May, August, or November. Special elections are held when a governing body feels that it just can't wait until the next scheduled general election. For example, as stated above, general elections for municipal governments are held during odd-numbered years. If something important enough arises, the governing body will not wish to wait for the next regular municipal election. It will opt for a special election. The cost of a special election is paid by the local governing body requesting it.

Partisan and Nonpartisan
Some public offices are filled by partisan election while others are filled by nonpartisan election. In a *partisan* election, the candidates are chosen by political parties; or to be more accurate, candidates are chosen by members of political parties. It is not unusual, for example, to hear or read about the Republican candidate for mayor or the Democratic candidate for county commissioner. Voters are required to reveal their party membership when voting on candidates during a primary election. The political party of each partisan candidate is shown on the primary, general, or special election ballot.

In a *nonpartisan* election the political parties are not directly involved. Is there a Democratic or Republican way to fight fires or repair streets? Those who favor nonpartisan local elections believe not.

Ohio state law requires partisan county elections. If a city does not have a charter, state law requires that city officials be elected on a partisan basis.

If a village does not have a charter, state law requires that village officials be elected on a nonpartisan basis. Nonpartisan elections are also held to fill township and school board positions. A municipal or county charter can provide for either partisan or nonpartisan elections.

Although political parties are not mentioned in either the federal or state constitutions, their role in our political system is established by federal and state law. One traditional role has been to sort out and endorse candidates. Where there is charter government, the people determine the role of political parties in their elections. One trend is noticeable: charters which establish the mayor-council form of government usually require partisan elections, while those which establish the council-manager form commonly call for nonpartisan elections.

Eligibility to Vote
You are qualified to vote if:

- You are a citizen of the United States.
- You are at least 18 years of age on or before the day of the general election. If you *will be* 18 on or before the day of the general election, you may vote in the primary election for candidates, but not issues.
- You will be a resident of Ohio for at least 30 days before the election.
- You register to vote at least 30 days before the election.

Your Vote Counts
Have you ever wondered whether your vote really makes any difference? It can. Here are a few actual examples from recent elections:

Table 3-3: Close Elections

Local Government (Year) Question on Ballot	Number of Votes Won By	Number of Votes Lost By
Orange Township (1999) Approve zoning plan?		2
Fostoria City (1999) Increase length of council terms?	Tie	Tie
Riverdale Local School District (1998) Approve 1% income tax?		2
Craig Beach Village (1998) Repeal income tax?	3	

Voter-Controlled Taxes
State law requires citizen approval of certain local laws before those laws can be enforced. This is, in effect, a requirement for an automatic referendum. (See Chapter 2 for more information on the

Similarities on the Local Level 41

referendum.) Tax laws are at the top of the list. Local governments have very little authority to levy or increase taxes without voter approval.

This is another example of democracy at the local level. Three of the better known voter-controlled local government taxes are upon property, income, and sales.

Property Tax
The *property tax* is used by local governments only. It is a tax on privately-owned real estate, public utility property, and personal property (such as machinery and equipment) used in business. All counties, townships, cities, villages, and school districts have the power to levy the property tax. Most of the money obtained from property taxes, however, goes to school districts. While small amounts of the tax can be levied without voter approval, most of the amount in force today (80 percent or more) has been authorized by the voters.

The reason that only small amounts can be levied without voter approval stems from a 1933 amendment to the state constitution. The total property tax rate — that is, the total of all levies by all local governments against a single property — was capped at 10 mills, and voter approval was (and still is) required for any amount over 10 mills. In 1933, each local government then levying the tax was allocated a proportional share of the 10 mills. Those few mills were theirs to use annually and for as long as they wished. A share of the 10 mills is referred to as *inside millage*. Anything in addition is called *outside millage* and it must be voter approved.

A *mill* is one-tenth of a cent. The total tax rate, which can be well over 50 mills, for a specific property is then applied to the assessed valuation of that property. *Assessed valuation* is the value placed on property for tax purposes, which is considerably lower than the market value. It is supposed to be 35 percent of market value. You can contact your county auditor for tax and assessment information on your home or any other property located in your county.

Property tax rates are not uniform throughout the state. Within legal restraints, each local government sets its own rate. Separate rates (municipal, school district, and so on) are then added together and the total rate is applied against the assessed value of property. So, the owner of a home with a market value of $90,000 might be charged $1,500 per year, while the owner of another home worth the same amount, but located in a different school district or a different city, might be charged more or less.

Charters can establish rules different from those set by state law. A charter can allow a municipal council to levy, without a vote of the people, rates higher than those established by state law. For example, a charter can provide that council can levy a property tax not exceeding six (or any other figure) mills without a further vote of the people. The thinking here is that when the voters approve the charter, they are also approving the higher maximum property tax rate. Without such a provision, council would have to seek voter approval for the higher rate (outside millage).

Income Tax

The *income tax* is a major source of municipal revenue. Income tax is a tax on money earned. A municipal council can tax the income of persons who live or work in the municipality. The Akron City Council, for example, can tax the income of persons who live or work in Akron. Ohio cities and villages began using the income tax over 60 years ago. The City of Toledo was the first. The number using the tax has increased from one in 1946 to near 550 in 2000.

State law allows cities and villages to levy an income tax of not more than one percent without a vote of the people. At one percent, a person earning $35,000 per year would pay $350 in taxes per year. Voters can authorize a rate of more than one percent, and by initiative or referendum they can reduce or even eliminate the tax. As is the case with the property tax rate, municipal charters can establish an income tax rate which can be levied without a further vote of the people. The charter rate can be higher than the one percent rate set by state statute.

By 2000, the income tax was used by 540 municipalities: 228 cities and 312 villages. Of that total, the rates of 21 municipalities were under 1.00 percent, rates of 425 were between 1.00 and 1.99 percent, and rates of 94 were 2.00 percent or higher. The highest rate was 2.50 percent levied by four cities. People approve a higher municipal income tax rate for a variety of reasons. Perhaps the income tax increase was offset by a reduction in the property tax rate. Or, perhaps the increased revenue was pledged to a widely recognized municipal need such as public safety equipment or construction projects.

The Ohio General Assembly allowed school districts to use the income tax in 1981, but changed its mind in 1983. During that brief period, voters in six districts approved tax levies ranging from one-half percent to one percent. However, in 1990 a new state law was passed which once again allowed school districts to levy an income tax (with voter approval). This "on again–off again–on again" history reflects some controversy. A general trend had been developing in which municipalities would depend primarily on the income tax and leave the property tax for the schools. This informal earmarking in principle of tax sources ended when schools entered the income tax field. Today, on the local level, school districts and municipalities compete for the income tax, and they also compete with other local governments for the property tax.

The Ohio Department of Taxation administers the school income tax program. It reported that for the year 1999, 120 of Ohio's 611 school districts levied an income tax.

Sales Tax

The *sales tax* is a major source of revenue for county governments. They share the sales tax field with the state and with transit authorities. Counties can levy a sales tax of not more than 1.5 percent upon most goods that people buy except medicine, uncooked foods, and other exempted items listed in state law. During any given year, there can be one or two counties not levying the sales tax. Voters give authority and voters take away.

Voters control the county sales tax. When all or any part of the first one percent is enacted by the county commissioners, citizens can place the issue on the ballot (referendum). When any amount over one percent is enacted, the issue automatically goes on the ballot.

A Word of Caution

There is a problem when voters can control local taxes but not state or federal taxes. Some people might vote against local taxes simply because they cannot vote against state or federal taxes. They show their objection to taxes in general by voting against the only ones they can vote against: those proposed by local government. This can and does damage local governments. A reflection of this situation is the number of times that some local governments, especially school boards, repeatedly place the *same* tax or bond issue on the ballot.

Public Records and Open Meetings

Ohio's Public Records and Open Meeting Laws give citizens the right to know what their state and local officials are doing. These laws give people the right to see or obtain copies of public records and to witness meetings of public bodies. As with any law, penalties are provided for violation. While the "right to know" is protected by law, it is comforting to know that it is seldom necessary to resort to legalities. Citizens can usually obtain copies of records or information about meetings by simply writing, calling, or visiting the office of their local government. Use the following contacts if you are not sure where to begin.

Table 3-4: Where to Locate Public Records

Local Government	Starting Place or Office
County	Commissioners' Office
Township	Township Clerk
City	City Clerk
Village	Village Clerk
School District	Treasurer

Public Records

A *record* is any form, letter, or other written material created by or received by a unit of government which deals with its day-to-day activities. A record is just about anything that is kept in file cabinets or stored in computers.

The Public Records Law requires that public records be open for public inspection, and allows people to obtain copies of public records. This does not mean, however, that all records kept by local governments are open to the public. Students, for example, need not worry that their school records will be shown to anyone who is simply interested. Exemptions listed in the Public Records Law are:

- Medical records;
- Adoption, probation, and parole records;
- Trial preparation records;
- Confidential law enforcement records;
- Records whose release is prohibited by state or federal law.

The last item in the list above casts considerable doubt on just what is or is not a public record. There isn't a person alive who knows what is in all the state and federal laws. This is a real problem for the government employee who receives a request to see a record. He or she is in danger of breaking either the Public Records Law or some other law every time a request is received. Take, for example, a request to see an employee's service record. Much of the information contained in the service record is public in nature. However, laws will be broken if the record is handed out and it contains material dealing with workers' compensation claims or participation in public assistance programs.

A person who asks to see or obtain a copy of a record can be required to submit a written request. This helps the government employee to respond correctly. The applicant can also be charged a reasonable fee for copies of material requested.

Questions concerning what is or what is not a public record should not discourage legitimate requests. Most of the records kept by local governments in Ohio are open and available to the public.

Open Meetings

Political deals, it is often said, are frequently made in darkened, smoke-filled rooms from which the public is excluded. Ohio's Open Meeting Law, also called the *Sunshine Law*, was created to prevent this. It was created to let the sunshine and the public into those "smoke-filled" rooms. To put it more accurately, the Sunshine Law is intended to keep elected decision makers from meeting in private. The Sunshine Law states:

> All meetings of any public body are declared to be public meetings open to the public at all times.

The law defines a local public body as any legislative authority or board, commission, committee, agency, or similar decision making body of any political subdivision, school district, or local public institution. Every meeting is subject to the Open Meeting Law if (1) it is pre-arranged, (2) if it is attended by a majority of the members of the group involved, and (3) if public business is discussed.

Any person can receive advance notice of public meetings. Requests should be made to the local government from which you want the notification. A reasonable fee can be charged for this service.

Executive Sessions

There are times when public officials can meet in private. Just as the Public Records Law does not require that all records be open to the public, the Sunshine Law does not require that all meetings be open to the public. The Sunshine Law lists specific reasons for which closed (closed to the public) meetings can be held. Closed meetings can be held to:

- Discuss individual employees;
- Consider the purchase or sale of property;
- Discuss legal matters with an attorney;
- Prepare for collective bargaining with a union;

- Consider security arrangements if information can be used for criminal purposes;
- Consider matters required by federal laws or rules or state statute to be kept confidential.

No formal action can be taken during an executive (closed) session. Action based on decisions arrived at during an executive session, such as approving a motion or introducing an ordinance, must be taken during a meeting open to the public.

While Ohio's Sunshine Law allows people to witness decision making, it can also impede understanding among the decision makers. The *real* reasons members side one way or another on an issue may never be known, even among the members. Some members, for example, might not wish to raise or discuss sensitive issues or to express personal beliefs in public. Consequently, since the law was passed in 1975, public officials have been less able to discover how their peers really feel about matters being considered. It is interesting to speculate whether the U.S. Constitution could have been developed during open meetings. Guards stood at the doors of the Constitutional Convention.

Land Use and Development

Imagine, for a moment, an urbanized community wherein the residents refuse to give up their individual freedom to use and to maintain their property as they see fit — allowing absolutely no governmental interference. We would encounter unplanned and unregulated neighborhoods, each with a mix of land uses. Yes, trucking terminals might be next to child day care centers and a heliport might be next to single family homes. Many buildings would be poorly constructed and/or dilapidated. In our imagination, we can paint an even more dismal picture. We would find chaotic conditions wherein few people would wish to live or invest their assets. Local government in Ohio has been given tools by which to regulate land use and development. Principle among those tools are: zoning, planning, subdivision regulations, and building regulations.

Zoning

In Ohio, zoning authority is available to both municipal and township governments. Zoning is used in all but the smallest municipalities and in about half of the townships — the most urbanized half.

A standard dictionary gives a half dozen or more definitions for the words *zone* and *zoning*. Those applicable here are: (1) an area in a city designated for a particular type of building, enterprise, or activity, and (2) to divide into zones. We in Ohio expand the definition to include not only cities, but also villages and townships. Who does the designating? The local governing body, based upon the recommendations of experts. How is the plan implemented? By making it law. A zoning ordinance (resolution) is just that: a local law.

There are two official zoning documents: the written law and a map. The map illustrates how the community is zoned. Looking at the map is the easiest way to determine how a specific place (for example, the lot upon which your home sits) is zoned. The zoning map shows specific areas or districts (called zones) and indicates the permitted land use within each area. The zoning classification around your home is probably *Residential* meaning that only various types of residential land uses are permitted in that area.

Population density is a major factor in determining how complex a community's land use (zoning) plan should be. Villages and townships with small populations might have only the basic *Residential, Commercial,* and *Industrial* zoning classifications. Larger communities have many more. Each classification has specifications dealing with such matters as building height, parking, fences, signs, and even front, side, and rear yard requirements.

The typical zoning statute makes provision for its management and enforcement. Ongoing enforcement is handled by the executive branch of the government. An employee, with a job title such as *Zoning Administrator*, is designated to conduct the office and field work. He or she usually has support staff. In addition, municipal councils are required to appoint a *Planning Commission* while township trustees appoint a *Zoning Commission*. By whatever name it is known, the commission oversees the operation of the zoning laws and, from time to time, recommends amendments.

A *Board of Zoning Appeals* is also appointed. Appeals to the board can be made by persons who disagree with a decision of the Zoning Administrator, or who request a variance (exception) to a requirement as it relates to their property. Decisions of the Board of Zoning Appeals can be appealed to the Court of Common Pleas.

Planning

Urban planning has become an essential part of local government. The broad scope of urban planning goes far beyond land use and zoning. It also encompasses traffic and transportation, leisure areas, water and sanitary sewer systems, and just about anything else having to do with current or projected living conditions. Many cities and villages have a Planning Department (sometimes called a Community Development Department) with professional staff while others obtain planning services from the private sector or from another governmental agency.

Planning for townships can be performed by the county planning commission or, if one exists, a regional planning commission. Services can also be obtained from the private sector. Multi-county planning commissions have been voluntarily formed in the major metropolitan areas. Membership is optional but highly desirable. Municipal governments and counties, most with but some without their own planning commissions, join in order to participate in and benefit from cooperative planning efforts.

The list of planning subjects handled by regional agencies is a long one. No single agency does it all but included is: planning for aging programs, air quality, criminal justice, economic development, energy, highway and transit, human resources, rural housing, solid waste disposal, and water quality. Much of the work stems from federal grant-in-aid programs.

✓ Did you know?

Regional planning agencies serve municipalities, counties, and townships in Ohio. They provide a variety of services, depending on local needs and state requirements. Here are the big four, each of which serve an area containing a population of 1,000,000 or more.

Miami Valley Regional Planning Commission
40 West Fourth Street, Suite 400
Dayton, Ohio 45402-1827
Phone: (937) 223-6323   Website: www.mvrpc.org
Counties served: Darke, Greene, Miami, Montgomery, and Preble

Mid-Ohio Regional Planning Commission
285 East Main Street
Columbus, Ohio 43215-5272
Phone: (614) 233-4101   Website: www.morpc.org
Counties served: Delaware, Fairfield, Fayette, Franklin, Licking, Pickaway, Ross, and Union

Northeast Ohio Areawide Coordinating Agency
1299 Superior Avenue
Cleveland, Ohio 44114-3024
Phone: (216) 241-2414   Website: www.noaca.org
Counties served: Cuyahoga, Geauga, Lake, Lorain, and Medina

Ohio-Kentucky-Indiana Regional Council of Governments
801-B West Eighth Street, Suite 400
Cincinnati, Ohio 45203-1610
Phone: (513) 621-6300   Website: www.oki.org
Counties served:
Ohio – Butler, Clermont, Hamilton, and Warren
Kentucky – Boone, Campbell, and Kenton
Indiana – Dearborn

Subdivision Regulations

Subdivision of what? Land. The next chapter tells that our newly formed federal government, in 1785, decided to survey the Northwest Territory into townships (36 square miles each) and sections (one square mile each). It was done to facilitate the buying and selling of land and to keep track of ownership.

A working definition of "subdivision" is the division of land into lots or building sites. The number of lots in a subdivision can run from just a few to several hundred. Typical lots intended for single family homes are usually about 70 feet wide and perhaps 120 feet deep.

Today, local subdivision regulations serve not only to facilitate commercial transactions but also to assure that new housing developments are constructed to be an asset to the community. To be an asset, adequate water lines, sanitary sewer lines, and storm sewer pipe must be laid. Also, streets, gutters, and sidewalks must be constructed. Minimum lot size is established. Some local governments also require street lighting, and a few specify underground cable television, electric, and phone lines.

A drawing (called preliminary plat) of the proposed subdivision must be submitted by the developer (land owner) and approved by the local government involved before a final plat is prepared. The final plat must also be approved before construction of public facilities (streets, etc.) can start. When construction is finished to the satisfaction of local building inspectors, signatures of local government officials are affixed to the final plat.

At that point, the local government assumes ownership of the rights-of-way and easements together with physical improvements such as streets and sewers. Only then will the plat be accepted by the County Recorder for filing. Building lots cannot be sold until the final plat is recorded.

Municipal and county governments have authority to adopt and enforce subdivision regulations. Township governments do not have this authority unless they are located in a county which does not regulate subdivision development.

Building Regulations
People are sometimes dismayed when they learn that a permit must be purchased before some kinds of work can be performed on their homes or other property. Permits are required for new construction and for modification of building structure, plumbing, electrical, or heating systems. If the bad news is that money must be paid for a permit, the good news is that the finished job will be inspected by a professional who will be on your side if questions arise concerning quality of work.

Building regulation is a wide field upon which state, county, and municipal governments participate. Townships can participate if their county government does not. Below is a summary description of the agencies and roles within building regulation.

The state Board of Building Standards, organizationally a part of the Ohio Department of Commerce, certifies (grants their seal of approval to) local building departments when they meet the standards established by the Board. The Board also tests and certifies the competence of local building inspectors.

For regulatory purposes, buildings in Ohio are grouped as (1) residential – i.e., one, two, or three family dwellings, or (2) commercial – i.e., everything else. State law leaves the regulation of residential construction and alterations to local governments. As a general rule, it can be assumed that practically all cities, many villages, and even a few townships have assumed responsibility for the safety of residential structures within their jurisdiction by establishing their own building departments. As an alternative, however, it is possible to turn the responsibility over to the county (assuming the county is agreeable). For example, Franklin County contains 17 townships and 25 municipalities. The Franklin County Building Department issues residential building permits and performs inspections for all 17 townships and for six small villages. The remaining 19 municipalities have their own building departments which are certified to control residential construction and alterations.

The BOCA National Building Code or a code similar to it is used to control residential construction. BOCA stands for Building Officials Conference of America. If enforcement disputes arise, builders can appeal decisions of building inspectors to a local board, usually the Board of Zoning Appeals.

State Law requires state government participation in the regulation of commercial construction and the Ohio Basic Building Code is the mandated guide.

Most of Ohio's larger-population cities and counties have building departments which are certified to regulate not only residential but also commercial construction. Where there are no such departments, oversight of commercial construction is provided by the Ohio Department of Commerce which maintains offices in Akron, Athens, Batavia, Reynoldsburg, and Toledo. Its Bureau of Plans and Specifications reviews building plans. Inspectors from its Bureau of Construction Compliance visit the job site to assure compliance with the Ohio Basic Building Code.

The Board of Building Appeals, also organizationally within the Ohio Department of Commerce, considers appeals made to adjudication orders (stop work orders or differences in interpretation of the Ohio Basic Building Code) issued by state or local building inspectors. The Board can reverse, modify, or repeal the order.

Chapter 3 Review

■ Summary

The variety of functions described in this chapter are not directly related to one another but they are all attributes of local government. Some of the things that local governments have in common include: structure, elections, public records and open meetings, voter-controlled taxes, and the ability to control land use and development.

Structure. All local governments have governing bodies and executive branches. Within constraints set by state law, the governing body establishes policy; that is, it decides what the local government will do. Governing bodies are known as boards of county commissioners, boards of township trustees, city councils, village councils, and boards of education. When it has the ability to enact laws, the governing body is also a legislative body. The executive branch carries out policies established by the governing body. Only municipal and county governments have a judicial branch.

Elections. Voters select candidates and decide issues for all three levels of government on election day. There are three types of elections: primary, general, and special.

The major purpose of a primary elections is to select candidates. Primaries are held in May. General elections are held each November. General elections for federal, state, and county governments are held during even-numbered years. General elections for local governments other than county are held in odd-numbered years. Special elections can be held in February, May, August, or November.

Ohio state law requires partisan elections for county and non-charter city offices. It requires nonpartisan elections for villages without charters and for townships and school districts. A charter can require either partisan or nonpartisan elections.

You are qualified to vote at age 18 if you are a U.S. citizen, have been a resident of Ohio at least 30 days prior to the election, and have been registered to vote in the precinct in which you reside at least 30 days before the election.

Voter-Controlled Taxes. Voters have a great deal of control over local taxes. They do not have the same control over state and federal taxes. Major sources of revenue on the local level are: (1) the *property tax* for school districts, townships, and to a lesser extent, counties and municipalities; (2) the *sales tax* for counties, and (3) the *income tax* for municipal governments. School districts have recently gained entry into the income tax field.

Public Records and Open Meetings. The best way to obtain information about local government is simply to ask for it. You may contact the county commissioners' office, township clerk, city or village clerk, and treasurer of the school board. However, should that fail, state law stipulates that most records are available to the public and that most meetings of elected public officials and other decision makers are also open to the public.

Land Use and Development. Local government in Ohio has been given tools by which to regulate land use and development. Principle among those tools are: zoning, planning, subdivision regulations, and building regulations.

Zoning designates permitted land uses. Major land use classifications are residential, commercial, and industrial. The zoning map illustrates the zoning law. Zoning is used in all but the smallest municipalities and it is also found in about half of the townships. No other local law has greater influence in the urban environment.

Planning. The term "planning" when used in respect to local government is the systematic study of just about anything that affects the urban environment. Among other things, a planning study of current and recommended land uses determines the features of a zoning plan.

Subdivision Regulations. Local subdivision regulations assure that new housing developments are an asset to the community. This is accomplished by requiring adequate public facilities–i.e., streets, utilities, and so forth.

Building Regulations. Building regulations protect public health and safety by assuring that new buildings are constructed well, and that repairs and modifications are properly performed. Oversight is maintained by the Ohio Board of Building Standards. County and municipal building departments issue building permits and conduct compliance inspections. Where there is no certified local department, commercial building permits are issued and compliance inspections are conducted by employees of the Ohio Department of Commerce.

■ Glossary

Annual Budget. The yearly estimates of revenues and expenditures. Also, a plan dealing with how revenue is generated and how it is spent.

Assessed Valuation. The value placed on property for tax purposes. In Ohio, 35 percent of market value.

Election. The settling of matters by ballot.

Executive Branch. That part of a governmental organization which carries out (executes) policies established by the governing body.

Governing Body. That part of a governmental organization which establishes policy to be carried out by the executive branch.

Income Tax. A tax on wages and other compensation.

Judicial Branch. That part of a governmental organization containing one or more courts.

Legislative Branch. A governing body which can enact laws. A legislature.

Mill. One-tenth of a cent. A term used in reference to the property tax.

Nonpartisan. Not involving political parties.

Open Meeting. A meeting open for attendance by persons who are not members of the group holding the meeting.

Partisan. Political or involving political parties

Plat. A map showing details of lots, streets, alleys, public grounds, utilities, etc.

Property Tax. A tax on privately-owned real estate, public utility property, and personal property (such as machinery and equipment) used in business.

Public Records. Records developed and maintained by a

Similarities on the Local Level 57

government.

Sales Tax. A tax on most goods that people buy. In Ohio, medicine and uncooked foods are exempt.

Subdivision. As used in local government, the dividing of land into building lots.

Zoning. The designation of permissible land uses in defined areas or districts.

■ Review Questions

1. Can all governing bodies enact laws?
2. Are general elections for local governments other than counties held in odd or even numbered years?
3. What kinds of local governments must have partisan elections?
4. The income tax is the major source of revenue for what kind of local government?
5. The sales tax can be levied by what kind of local government?
6. Are all governmental records open for public inspection?
7. Are all local government meetings open to the public?
8. Do all township governments have authority to develop and enforce subdivision regulations?
9. What state agency certifies the competency of local building departments and inspectors?
10. (True or false) Local government members of regional planning commissions can be located in more than one county.

Answers to Review Questions: 1. No; 2. Odd; 3. County and non-charter cities; 4. Municipal; 5. County; 6. No; 7. No; 8. No; 9. Ohio Board of Building Standards; 10. True.

Chapter 4: MANAGING IN THE WILDERNESS

The Surveyed Township

When independence from Great Britain was finally won, and after peace with Native American tribes was in sight, the new United States of America found itself the owner of an enormous amount of land. Newly acquired land, known as the Northwest Territory because it was located northwest of the Ohio River, seemed to stretch endlessly into the unknown wilderness.

The Continental Congress (1774–1788) wanted settlers to move into the wilderness lands. It felt that the country would grow and prosper with the spread of farming and the establishment of commercial centers. Ambitious plans were made. Most of the land would be sold, resulting in private ownership and producing much-needed revenue for the new government. It was also planned that a considerable amount of land would be given away in the form of land grants to stimulate development and settlement. Grants of land would be used in many ways: to reward army veterans; to encourage the development of schools, colleges, roads, canals, and religion; and to satisfy other congressional ambitions.

Land Grants

Land was given to army veterans in payment for their military service. Non-commissioned solders were entitled to 100 acres; ensigns, 150 acres; lieutenants, 200 acres; captains, 300 acres; majors, 400 acres; lieutenant colonels, 450 acres; colonels, 500 acres; brigadier generals, 850 acres; and major generals, 1,100 acres. George Washington was entitled to 23,333 acres which he never claimed.

Grants of land were given for schools, colleges, roads, and canals. Eventually, 704,202 acres were given as Ohio school lands. The fate of the Ohio School Lands Program is revealed in Chapter 10. Over 46,000 acres contributed to the establishment of Ohio University. More than 1,100,000 acres were donated by Congress as Ohio canal lands. These were sold by the state for $2,257,487 to pay construction costs. Ebenezer Zane received a grant of 1,929 acres to lay out a road from Wheeling, (now West) Virginia through Ohio to Maysville, Kentucky. Known as "Zane's Trace," the road connected Cambridge, Zanesville, Lancaster, and Chillicothe.

Religion was also encouraged with land grants. Grants of ministerial lands totaling 43,525 acres were made in the portion of the Northwest Territory which is now Ohio. The program, which operated in relatively few townships, was managed by the trustees of those townships. Ministerial lands within their township were leased and the resulting revenue was supposed to be used to encourage religion, presumably by donating it to churches in the township. Ohio is the only state where Congress gave land for the support of religion, except for a few small missions in the West. The program was not managed well and never amounted to much. In 1833, Congress allowed the state government to sell the ministerial lands, invest the money, and pay the interest until 1968 (135 years!) to churches which were, in 1833, participating in the program. In 1968, Ohio voters decided that any future income from that source would be used for educational purposes.

Neither sales nor grants could take place, however, until some way was found to keep track of land transactions. How could a person, for example, buy 160 acres of wilderness land unless he and everybody else could determine the exact location of those acres? Settlers in the areas south of the Northwest Territory often found themselves involved in a nightmare of conflicting claims for the same parcel of land. To claim land, they described the location by wooden stakes, slashes on trees, and landmarks such as rivers, streams, or outcropping rock. Clearly, the settlers needed to find a better way to describe their land. Thomas Hutchins, Geographer of the United States, is given much of the credit in finding that better way. Today, we do not have a United States Geographer. The

Continental Congress, however, needed such a professional when trying to understand the huge, largely unexplored, land mass which was later to become the 48 contiguous United States.

Thomas Hutchins

In the year 1781, Thomas Hutchins, a surveyor by profession, was appointed Geographer of the United States. (A *surveyor* establishes locations and boundaries by using mathematical principles to measure straight, curved, and angled lines.) He recommended surveying the entire Northwest Territory (a land area of about 250,000 square miles) in order to subdivide the entire expanse into squares called *townships*. The surveyed townships could then be used to locate specific parcels of land. The recommendation was adopted by Congress and Hutchins personally conducted the first land survey made in the Northwest Territory. Since the surveyed townships evolved into local governments, Thomas Hutchins occupies a significant niche in the history of township government.

History books do not tell us very much about Thomas Hutchins, although his colorful life certainly deserves mention. His childhood ended when, at age 15, his parents died. This was in 1745 — long before the American Revolution. All that we know about his childhood is that he received a good education. His family must have been well-off because there were no free public schools in those days. Hutchins left his New Jersey home and joined the British Army. We can only speculate about the reason; perhaps he had no other family or means of support.

Because of his education, Hutchins was given the rank of ensign in His Majesty's Royal American Regiment. He was appointed paymaster, an officer who pays wages and keeps records of the payments. He steadily climbed the career ladder. At age 28, Lieutenant Hutchins was appointed quartermaster, the officer in charge of the supply of food, clothing, and equipment for the soldiers. Still later, at age 33, Captain Hutchins served as assistant engineer. In that position he became a student and master of surveying.

His Majesty's Royal American Regiment fought in the *French and Indian War*, which took place between 1754 and 1763. The regiment later attempted to provide safety for settlers throughout the American wilderness. Wherever the army went, the surveyor was kept busy establishing routes, laying out forts, and most importantly, making maps.

Surveyors and map makers could become quite famous in those days, as a map of a far away or unfamiliar place was a prize to cherish. And, maps had great military value! Hutchins' maps became known on both sides of the Atlantic Ocean.

On the eve of the American Revolution, Hutchins was in London, England making arrangements for the printing and sale of his newest map. He described the map as covering 500,000 square miles of the interior parts of North America. His advertisement stated that the map included "the great rivers Mississippi and Ohio, the lakes Erie, Huron, and Michigan, as well as the Indian nations."

Not wishing to fight against his native country, he resigned from the British Army when the American Revolution began. London was not a good place for an American to be in 1776. Hutchins was accused of being a spy when he tried to send a letter to Benjamin Franklin who was in Paris, France (Franklin was, at the time, American Ambassador to France).

Hutchins was jailed, his papers seized, and all of his money taken away. He was held for six weeks in what has been described as a "dark dungeon." When he was finally released, nothing was given back to him. Nevertheless, with the help of friends, he was able to make his way to France and then back to America where he joined the American army.

At age 51, Hutchins was appointed Geographer of the United States by the Continental Congress. His ideas were written into the Land Ordinance of 1785, which required the use of township surveys in the Northwest Territory. While being protected from the Native American tribes by army troops, he personally conducted the first survey which followed the rules established by that law. That first survey is known as the *Seven Ranges*.

After a lifetime of service as an army officer, explorer, surveyor, and engineer on the frontier, he died at age 59 in Pittsburgh, Pennsylvania. History makes no mention of a wife or children. His grave has been lost, but the results of his work are

Managing in the Wilderness 63

very much with us today. In Ohio, there are 1,309 townships which contain local governments.

The Land Ordinance of 1785

The *Land Ordinance of 1785* established the rules for the orderly surveying, sale, and settlement of public lands. Land could not be sold or occupied until it had been surveyed and the survey accepted by the federal government. The Land Ordinance called for surveyed townships and set the size of each at six miles square, which totals 36 square miles. Each square mile (which is also 640 acres) was called a *section*.

Figure 4-1: Ohio's Major Land Surveys

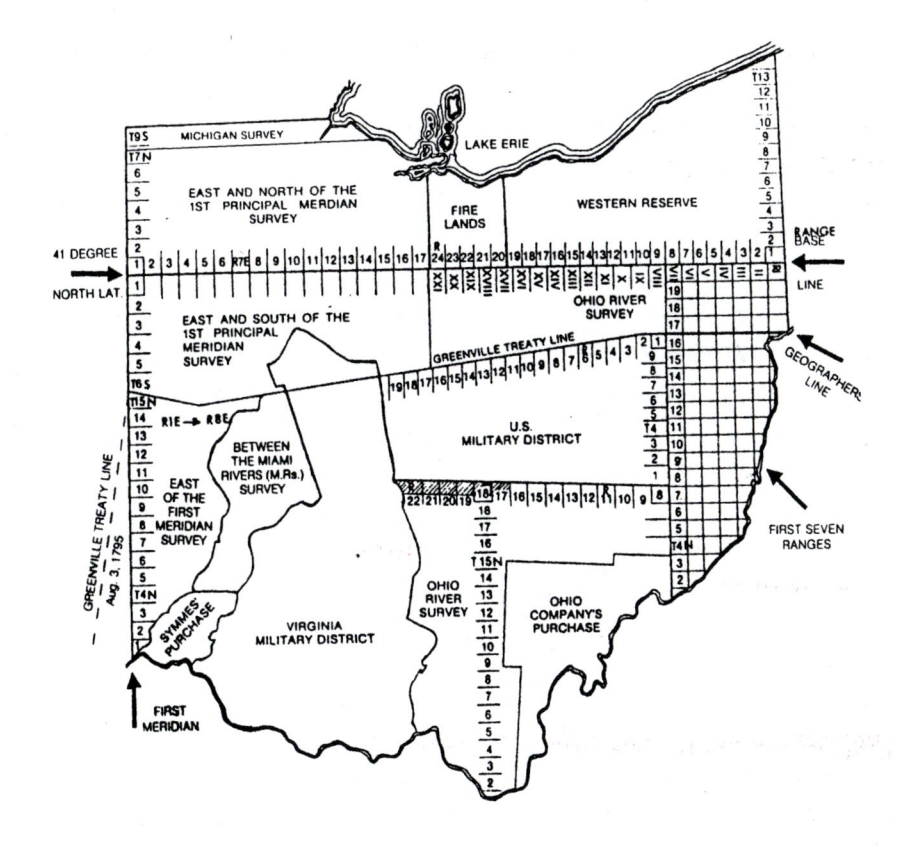

Within each survey, townships and all sections inside the township were numbered. Thus, the location of land could be pinpointed right down to a quarter section (160 acres) or less of a specific township. A quarter section could be described, for example, as the northwest quarter of Section 17, Township 3, of a particular survey.

It took several surveys to cover the land area which is now Ohio. Each survey was given a unique and distinctive name. Some names, such as the U.S. Military District and the Virginia Military District indicate the purpose of the survey. Both surveys were of lands intended for military veterans. Two other surveys were of large land purchases by private interests: the Ohio Company's Purchase and the Symmes' (John Cleves Symmes) Purchase. The Fire Lands Survey was of lands set aside for persons who had lived in seven towns burned by the British during the Revolutionary War.

The name of the first survey, the Seven Ranges, is also descriptive. Vertical rows of townships are called *ranges*. The survey started where the Ohio River crossed the Pennsylvania border and went 42 miles due west. Each range is six miles across and there were seven ranges.

> ✓ **Did you know?**
> In 1877, all federal land surveys, notes and related material dealing with Ohio lands were placed in the care of the State of Ohio. These records are maintained in the State Archives by the Ohio Historical Society, 1982 Velma Avenue, Columbus, Ohio 43211. Phone: (614) 297-2500. Website: www.ohiohistory.org. The staff responds to inquiries from genealogists, students and other interested persons. Published material is available upon request.

Over the years, Congress passed a series of land acts that allowed variations to the township survey system as established in the Land Ordinance of 1785. In the Ohio Territory, a five mile

Managing in the Wilderness   65

square township was occasionally substituted for the six mile square township and townships were not required to be square in the Virginia Military District. However, most of the surveys in the Northwest Territory followed the same general pattern.

The Civil Township

As used to describe a township, the word *civil* means government — that is, township with government. A few civil townships were established by the territorial government before Ohio became a state. The townships were in the vicinity of what is now Washington County. Those first civil townships were re-established and more were created after Ohio achieved statehood. The state legislature decided, in 1804, to require civil townships throughout Ohio. When a surveyed township's population reached 80, its residents could form a township government. There can be little doubt concerning the popularity of civil townships at the close of the 18th century. Thomas Jefferson called them, "little republics." "These little republics," he predicted, "will be the main strength of the big one." In other words, civil townships would be the building blocks of the national government.

Original Responsibilities

At the close of the 18th century, difficult travel conditions separated settlers from their county government. Civil townships were created to fill the gap between the people and county government and thus to bring government closer to the people. What jobs were the civil townships created to perform? The following duties were listed in the 1841 edition of a book entitled, *Statutes of the State of Ohio of a General Nature*.

   (1) *Keep the Peace.* One justice of the peace (a minor judge) and a number of constables (police) were elected.
   (2) *Maintain Roads.* One highway supervisor was elected.
   (3) *Settle Boundary Disputes*. Three fence viewers were elected.

(4) *Poor Relief.* Two overseers of the poor were elected.
(5) *Manage Civil Township Affairs.* Three trustees, a clerk and a treasurer were also elected. An important task performed by the clerk was to record cattle brands.

The settlers could expect law and order from their township government. They could also expect roads and help in determining property boundaries. Most importantly, civil townships allowed settlers to control and manage their own local government. The seeds of Thomas Jefferson's little republics quickly sprouted throughout the states of the Northwest Territory. Elsewhere, however, the spread of civil townships slowed and came to a stop. Changed conditions reduced the need for civil townships. What changed? Technology.

> ✓ **Did you know?**
> A *Justice of the Peace* is minor judge with authority to keep the peace and settle small claims cases. The Justice of the Peace system was brought to this country by English colonists. It has been criticized for two reasons:
> - There is no requirement that justices have any sort of legal training; and
> - The justice's compensation is based on the fines he imposes.
>
> The Justice of the Peace system in Ohio was abolished in 1958 and replaced with county courts.
>
> A note of interest: the infamous Texas Judge Roy Bean, known as the "only law west of the Pecos" during the 1850s was a justice of the peace.

The Impact of Technology

During the early 1800s, the speed of transportation and the speed of communication were the same. Both traveled at the rate of about three miles per hour during good weather. Letters were transported

Managing in the Wilderness 67

by horse or boat. We can only imagine the isolation felt by settlers in the wilderness. In this situation, little governments (civil townships) were established close to the people to provide a sense of community. However, the situation quickly changed in a way that nobody living during Thomas Jefferson's lifetime (1743–1826) could have imagined. Several of these changes are outlined below.

Changes in Transportation

Canals. Ohio's canal system was started in 1825 and finished in 1847. The Ohio and Erie Canal connected Cleveland and Portsmouth. The Miami and Erie Canal ran between Toledo and Cincinnati. Manpower, animal power, and dynamite created ditches six feet deep throughout the state. Engineering marvels, the sloping sides were 26 feet apart at the bottom and 40 feet apart at the top. A level towpath was built along the side. On that path, a single horse could tow a fully loaded barge (flat bottom boat) weighing several thousand pounds.

Roads. Zane's Trace was finished in 1798, but Ohio's present-day road system was started in 1825. The National Road, which was constructed by the federal government to span the entire country, reached Zanesville in 1826, Columbus in 1833, and Springfield in 1838. By 1840, it crossed the entire state from east to west. Over the years, log and rock construction was replaced by asphalt and concrete construction. The National Road eventually became known as U.S. Route 40, much of which is still in use today.

Railroads. Canal transportation was soon overtaken by the railroads. When the Ohio and Erie Canal was completed between Cleveland and Portsmouth, less than 50 miles of railroad track had been laid in Ohio. By 1850, the length of train rails had grown to 300 miles. Toledo and Sandusky were early railroad towns. When the Civil War began in 1861, there were over 2,700 miles of track in Ohio. On the national level, railroads reached from the eastern coast to the Mississippi River by 1855 and to the Pacific coast by 1869.

Steamboats. Steamboats improved to the point where heavy ships could move upstream almost as easily as they could travel on lakes and oceans. Large rivers such as the Mississippi and Ohio

Rivers became highways for ships.

Changes in Communication
The telegraph was invented in 1837. The telegraph was a device which sent electrical impulses along wires strung from the sending point to the receiving point. A short impulse was a "dot" and a longer impulse was a "dash." Telegraph language was a code consisting of dots and dashes. The first long-distance message was sent from Washington D.C. to Baltimore, Maryland in 1844.

An exciting episode in the field of communications took place in 1860 when the Pony Express was established. Riders on horseback traveled between St. Joseph, Missouri, and Sacramento, California. Galloping at breakneck speeds through the wild west, they were able to cover the 2,000 miles in about eight days. The record delivery time was seven days and 17 hours. The life of the Pony Express was cut short when the first transcontinental telegraph line was completed in 1861, thus rendering the horse and rider obsolete as messengers. Technology in the field of communications soon advanced further when the telephone was invented in 1876.

The Declining Popularity of Civil Townships
Largely because of the advances in transportation and communication, the prediction of Thomas Jefferson failed to materialize. Civil townships did not become the building blocks of the national government. As better ways to travel and communicate were developed, the need for little governments close to their constituents faded. Today, 29 states including California, Florida, and Texas have no civil townships.

Why then were civil townships created in the Northwest Territory even as events were unfolding which negated the need for them? On the one hand, technological changes were unpredictable and they took place, one at a time, over a period of many years. On the other hand, plans for the settlement of the Northwest Territory were developed early on, as reflected in such documents as the Land Ordinance of 1785 and the Northwest Ordinance of 1787. The Congress carried out those plans.

Chapter 4 Review

■ Summary

The Continental Congress made ambitious plans for the colonization of the Northwest Territory. Most of the land would be sold to (1) achieve private ownership, and (2) obtain funds for the new U.S. Treasury. However, some land would be given away in the form of land grants to stimulate development and settlement.

A method to enable buyers and sellers to identify specific parcels of land was developed and legislated into law. The Land Ordinance of 1785 called for surveys to divide the entire territory into square parts called townships. One square mile (one 36th of most townships) from each township was set aside for the support of schools. Townships played two historical roles. First, the surveyed townships enabled people to keep track of land transactions. Second, those same surveyed townships were later turned into local governments. Civil townships provided rudimentary local government services to settlers in the Northwest Territory.

Thomas Hutchins played an important role in developing surveyed townships. His colorful career as a soldier, surveyor, map maker, and Geographer for the U.S. Congress also included being chief contributor to the township plan written into the Land Ordinance of 1785. He personally conducted the first survey in the Ohio Territory.

Thomas Jefferson was an enthusiastic supporter of civil townships. In fact, he referred to them as "little republics" which would form the foundation upon which the national government would rest.

As the 19th century unfolded, great changes in transportation and communication took place. Canal boats, railroads, and steamboats made travel faster and less difficult. Trails were turned into primitive roads. The telegraph and later the telephone sent messages over great distances in practically no time at all. When better ways to travel and communicate were developed, the need for little governments in each township faded. As the country expanded beyond the Northwest Territory, most of the new states developed without civil townships.

■ Glossary

Continental Congress. The legislative and governing body of the American colonies from 1774 until 1788.

French and Indian War. That part of the war between France and England (1754–1760), waged in America, in which the French received support from Native American allies. France lost its claim to the Northwest Territory and other lands in North America.

Justice of the Peace. A minor judge with authority to keep the peace and settle small claims cases.

Land Grant. A gift of land from the federal government to encourage development and settlement of wilderness areas.

Land Ordinance of 1785. The federal law which divided the Northwest Territory into square parts called townships. One square mile from each township was set aside to benefit schools.

Northwest Territory. The region awarded to the United States by England in 1783, at the close of the American Revolution, extending from the Great Lakes to the Ohio River between Pennsylvania and the Mississippi River.

Territorial Government. Temporary government established by Congress to rule until the Northwest Territory achieved statehood.

Managing in the Wilderness

■ Review Questions

1. Why was it necessary to survey the wilderness area known as the Northwest Territory?
2. The surveyed townships resulted from what federal law?
3. Who conducted the first survey in the Ohio Territory?
4. How many square miles are in a typical surveyed township?
5. Name at least three purposes for which land grants were given.
6. What were surveyed townships turned into?
7. List at least three duties performed by the early township governments.
8. Was Thomas Jefferson a friend or foe of civil townships?
9. Did the development of better ways to travel and communicate increase or decrease the need for civil townships?
10. Do most of the 50 states have civil townships?

Answers to Review Questions: 1. To enable buyers and sellers to identify specific parcels of land; to enable them to keep track of land transactions; 2. Land Ordinance of 1785; 3. Thomas Hutchins; 4. 36; 5. As payment for military service and for canals, schools, colleges, roads, and to encourage religion; 6. Civil townships; 7. Any three of the following: keep the peace, maintain roads, settle boundary disputes, poor relief, and manage township affairs; 8. Friend; 9. Decrease; 10. No.

Chapter 5: TOWNSHIP GOVERNMENT TODAY

Introduction

Civil townships are a part of the permanent organization of state government. They are territorial and political subdivisions of the state which were created to tend to the needs of 19th century society (which, in Ohio, was predominantly rural). Even though the state legislature, in response to changing circumstances, has gradually increased their capabilities, civil townships remain what they were originally intended to be: servants of the state. They can do only what the state legislature allows them to do. As we shall see later in this chapter, however, they are breaking out of that mold and becoming more like municipal governments.

Census Data

Census Bureau estimates for the year 1999 are used in this chapter. The Bureau, in 1999, listed 1,309 Ohio civil townships. This compares with 1,316 listed in 1990. The seven fewer are accounted for as follows:

Cuyahoga County: Warrensville Township incorporated to become the Village of Highland Hills (with parts distributed to abutting municipalities).

Licking County: Lima Township merged into Village of Pataskala.

Montgomery County: Madison Township merged into City of Trotwood. Randolph Township merged into Village of Clayton. Mad River Township merged into Village of Riverside.

Summit County: Green Township merged into Village of Green. Hudson Township merged into Village of Hudson.

At decade's end, there were 5,485,556 people living in Ohio civil townships – almost half of the total population of the state. That figure, however, needs explaining. Because many townships overlap municipal borders, there are people who live in both a township and a municipality at the same time. In most – perhaps all – Ohio counties, the total township population added to the total municipal population *exceeds* the total county population.

The average population per civil township is 4,190 (up from 4,058 in 1990). Roughly three-fourths have populations of less than 4,190, while about one-fourth have more. Those with larger populations are no longer entirely rural in nature. Table 5-1 lists the population figures for the civil townships which can be classified as quasi-urban, or at least moving in that direction.

Table 5-1: Number of Quasi-Urban Townships by Population Class 1990 and 1999

Population	Number of Townships (1990)	Number of Townships (1999)
4,058 to 10,000	209	
4,193 to 10,000		209
10,001 to 20,000	72	76
20,001 to 30,000	21	16
30,001 to 40,000	15	11
Over 40,000	8	13

Township Government Today

The townships with the largest populations are listed in Table 5-2, below.

Table 5-2: Townships with the Largest Populations

Township	County	1990 Population	1999 Population
Colerain	Hamilton	56,781	60,775
Green	Hamilton	52,687	54,847
Plain	Stark	49,181	51,883
Union	Butler	39,703	50,664
Washington	Montgomery	46,609	49,588
Marion	Marion	43,564	44,457
Sylvania	Lucas	39,983	44,122
Miami	Montgomery	40,700	43,821
Beavercreek	Greene	35,536	42,710
Boardman	Mahoning	40,700	41,708
Anderson	Hamilton	39,939	41,372
Bath	Greene	38,277	41,073
Deerfield	Warren	26,359	40,602

At the other extreme, some townships have very small populations. There are only 69 people in Jefferson Township (Guernsey County), 127 people in Brookfield Township (Noble County), and 154 people in Manchester Township (Morgan County).

When identifying a township, it is necessary to also identify the county within which it is located. While no two townships are named alike in a single county, many are named alike throughout the state. There are 19 names used 10 or more times. Names most frequently used are: Washington (43), Jackson (37), Union (27), Perry (26), Liberty (25), and Jefferson (24).

The Dual Role of Township Trustees

The modern civil township government has only four elected officials: three trustees and a clerk. These officials serve on a part-time basis. Elections for four-year terms are held during odd-numbered years. Terms are *staggered*; that is, they do not all end at the same time. Two trustees are elected and, the next time, one trustee and a clerk are elected.

Township trustees have two jobs. First, they are members of the governing body. As such, they decide, within the confines of state law, what the township government will do. The governing body is called the *board of township trustees*. Second, the trustees are also responsible for getting things done — that is, for executing the policies they have created. Thus, the township trustees are also members of the executive branch.

We can use the task of snow removal to illustrate the dual policy-executive role. If the board makes the policy decision that township roads will be kept clear of snow, it is up to the executive branch to get the job done. Perhaps the township has employees to do the job, or perhaps the township has contracted with a third party for snow removal services. If so, fine; if not, somewhere out there on cold, snowy nights, the township trustees themselves will be operating the snow plows. As members of the executive branch, they are directly responsible for the removal of the snow.

Township Clerk

The *township clerk* is the other elected official in the civil township government. The clerk serves as the general secretary to the board of trustees, is the township fiscal officer, and carries out additional duties as prescribed by state law. Additional duties include, for example, notifying the county board of elections of vacancies in elected offices or of changes in township boundaries.

The Expanding Scope of Activities

As stated in Chapter 4, townships had a limited number of duties to perform in 1841. As we shall see, the original duties have changed

Township Government Today 77

dramatically.

Original Tasks

Keeping the Peace. Township governments no longer have a judicial branch. Judicial services are provided by county or municipal courts. In addition, constables (police) are no longer elected, but may be hired by township trustees. State law also allows the trustees to contract with other townships, with a municipality, or with a county for police services. In addition, trustees can form a special police district. Such a district is actually another local government. It can cover all or only part of the township. Owners of land within the district are taxed to finance the police services.

Maintaining Roads. Even though the elected position, highway supervisor, has been eliminated, a highway superintendent or someone with a similar job title can be hired by the trustees. Today, Ohio civil townships have the responsibility of maintaining over 39,000 miles of road.

Settling Boundary Disputes. The elected fence viewer position has also been eliminated. Current state law requires the following: "The owners of adjoining lands shall build, keep up, and maintain in good repair, in equal shares, all partition fences between them, unless otherwise agreed upon by them in writing and witnessed by two persons." Township trustees are the referees in disputes about partition fences between neighbors. The law does not apply inside cities or villages or to land which has been subdivided into building lots.

Providing Relief for the Poor. Township governments no longer provide relief for the needy; this is handled by the county government.

Managing Township Affairs. The elected position, treasurer, has been eliminated. Treasurer duties are handled by the elected clerk.

The number of township activities would be quite limited if the 1841 listing had not been expanded. Services provided by today's townships would consist merely of police protection, road maintenance, and settlement of disputes over partition fences.

Increased Capabilities

It is possible, even necessary, to be highly self-sufficient when living in a rural area. The same is not true when living in an urban area. Urban dwellers are quite interdependent when it comes to matters of public health, safety, and well being. As population density increased, the Ohio General Assembly responded by gradually allowing township governments to provide additional services and by providing a variety of ways to furnish those services. Services can be provided (1) by the township government itself, (2) by contract with other local governments or private companies, or (3) by creating or joining a special purpose district.

Townships today can provide or obtain a wide variety of services, including (but not limited to) fire protection, ambulance and emergency medical services, cemeteries, street lighting, trash collection and disposal, hospitals, parks and playgrounds, water supply, waste water disposal, and zoning. The trustees can hire an administrator to manage the township's business. They can also provide library services, participate in federal grant-in-aid programs, and operate recreation centers. The increased ability to provide or obtain services has allowed township governments to cope with urbanization.

Special Districts

Ohio statutes authorize a variety of local governments which provide a single service (see Table 5-3 below). Each service requires the establishment of a *special district* (sometimes called a *special purpose district*) in which the single service can be provided. A special district can include two or more existing local governments, a portion of one existing local government, or some mixture of the two. This flexibility allows the targeting of a service area without regard to county, township, or municipal boundaries. Providing a service which otherwise would be unavailable is the positive side of special districts. The negative side is the complexity added to the overall field of local government. Residents can be quite uninformed concerning what special districts are, or for that matter, that they even exist. Special districts are inconspicuous governments.

Township Government Today

Some of the special districts listed in Table 5-3 can be created by the local governing bodies involved. Others are initiated by citizen petition directed to the common pleas or probate court. Once formed, a special district has its own governing body. That governing body can, with voter approval, levy taxes and incur debt.

School districts are, technically, special districts. Their single service is education. However, due to their significance and widespread existence, the U.S. Bureau of the Census and most political scientists give school districts a separate classification.

Table 5-3: Special Districts

Following is a partial listing of the types of special districts which can be created or joined to provide services to the residents of civil townships:

Ambulance	Police	Transit authority
Fire	Port authority	Union cemetery
Health	Recreation	Waste disposal
Hospital	Road	Water and sewer
Parks	Sanitary	

Who Is In Charge Here?

The desire of township trustees to govern in urban places and the willingness of the state legislature to let them do so can force residents to deal with a large number of service providers. As previously indicated, state law makes it possible for the residents of a civil township to receive services (1) from the township government itself, (2) from other local governments or private companies pursuant to contractual arrangements with the township government, or (3) from a special purpose district. Residents can find themselves being served and billed by not only the township, but also by other local governments, private companies, and special districts. If some needs are still unmet, residents must locate and make their own arrangements with private companies. Residents can find it awkward to do business with so many service providers.

Generally speaking, the problem of fragmented service delivery grows as urbanization increases.

Limited Self-Government (1991)

The terms *Self-Government* and *Home Rule* mean the same thing. They both refer to a government's ability to control its own affairs. Ohio townships had no such abilities until they were granted some in 1991, and more in 1999. For reasons known only to state legislators, the 1991 legislation used the term 'Self-Government' while the 1999 legislation used the term 'Home Rule.' By whatever name, the two statutes are interrelated.

The Ohio General Assembly, in 1991, made *Limited Self-Government* available to civil townships. With voter approval, civil townships could become a little more like municipal governments. The Board of Trustees became a legislative body! This was a major victory sought for decades by township trustees throughout the state. Why? More effective township government might stop the spread of municipal government. With the ability – however limited – to enact laws, civil townships became something more than mere servants of the state.

The 1991 legislation listed forbidden activities. Specifically, a township government could not enact laws that:
  (1) Change the township form of government in any way.
  (2) Establish, administer, or change construction or urban development laws, including:
     (a) subdivision regulations,
     (b) road construction standards,
     (c) water and sewer regulations,
     (d) urban sediment rules,
     (e) storm water or drainage regulations,
     (f) building standards and codes, and
     (g) other standard codes.
  (3) Enact laws dealing with major crimes, impose a fine of over $1,000, or impose a jail sentence.
  (4) Prohibit hunting or the sale or ownership of guns.

So, what could a township do with Limited Self-Government that it couldn't do without it? The answer lies in item (3) above. Townships can enact laws (called *resolutions*) dealing with minor crimes (called *misdemeanors*), and impose a fine of not more than $1,000. Minor crimes include such nuisances as excessive noise, trash and junk on private property, and the regulation of animals. Early actions by Plain Township (Stark County) dealt with the control of barking dogs and the parking of vehicles. Washington Township (Montgomery County) adopted an anti-noise resolution, and Sycamore Township (Hamilton County) adopted an animal control resolution. After a decade of use, Limited Self-Government had beneficial but minimal impact on township government. Township resolutions are not enforceable inside a municipality.

The cost of enforcing township resolutions is an additional tax burden. Most townships leave law enforcement to the county sheriff. With Limited Self-Government, however, the township was required to provide police to enforce its laws and an attorney to prosecute violators.

Limited Home Rule (1999)

Legislation (House Bill 187) which became effective on September 20, 1999, moved township government another step closer to becoming more like municipal government. The law expands the 1991 statute that gave townships Limited Self-Government.

The title "Home Rule" was officially substituted for "Self-Government." What's in a name? It's an ego booster. Now township advocates (like municipal advocates) can boast that they have Home Rule.

The traditional "one size fits all" attitude about laws controlling township governments was discarded. H.B. 187 divides townships into the following categories: (1) less than 5,000 population, (2) between 5,000 and 15,000, and (3) 15,000 or more. The count is of persons living in unincorporated areas of the township. Townships with a population of 15,000 or more will henceforth be known as "Urban Townships." Students of local government can expect that future General Assemblies will enact, from time to time, statutes dealing with single population categories. This follows the municipal village (less than 5,000 population) and city (5,000 or more) precedent.

Using 1999 Census estimated population numbers, the breakdown of townships within the H.B. 187 classification categories are as follow:

Table 5-4: Estimated Numbers of Townships within the H.B. 187 Classification Categories

Population (includes people inside municipalities)	Number of Townships
15,000 or more	60
5,000 to 15,000	217
Under 5,000	1,032
Total:	1,309

The trustees of a township having a population of 15,000 or more can adopt the Limited Home Rule form of government by resolution if the vote of the trustees is unanimous. Or, with a majority vote, the trustees can place the question on the ballot. The trustees of a township having a population between 5,000 and 15,000 can, by a majority vote, have the question placed on the ballot. Townships with populations of less than 5,000 are not permitted to adopt a Limited Home Rule form of government. The townships operating under the Limited Self-Government form were "grandfathered" into the Limited Home Rule form.

So, what can a township do with Limited Home Rule that it couldn't do under Limited Self-Government? H.B. 187 deals with several subjects but one stands out as being the most significant. The short answer is that townships operating under the Limited Home Rule form can engage in major public works activities and incur more debt in doing so.

The major changes brought about by H.B. 187 are in the realm of public works – i.e., construction, maintenance, and operation of physical facilities, including water and sewer systems. Trustees are authorized to retain consulting engineers and to carry out projects under the general (previously, 'direct') supervision of the County Engineer. Limited Home Rule townships can incur more debt than those without home rule. The debt limit for non-home rule townships is an amount equal to five percent of the township's assessed valuation (the value placed on land and improvements for tax purposes). The debt limit for home rule townships is ten and one-half percent of its assessed valuation. In addition, special assessments can be levied against properties which benefit from water and sewer improvements. This ability is a prize to be cherished because owners of township land usually annex to a municipality when they want dependable water and sewer service. In addition, trustees are given the authority to adopt and implement (but not to establish or revise – see below) regulatory codes (building, subdivision, etc.) provided that such adoption does not conflict with or duplicate programs conducted by the county government. Residents have the initiative and referendum to restrain any excessive zeal in the use of the new powers by the trustees.

The form of government is, however, still limited. Townships are not allowed to:
- increase, decrease, or otherwise alter the powers and duties of a township;
- except in regard to water and sewer service, enact laws dealing with major crimes, impose a fine of over $1,000, or impose a jail sentence;
- establish or revise subdivision regulations, road construction standards, sewer regulations, urban sediment rules, or storm water and drainage regulations;
- establish or revise building standards, building codes, and other standard codes;
- establish or revise water or sewer regulations except pursuant to state law; or
- establish regulations affecting hunting, fishing, or the possession, use, or sale of firearms.

Where the word "establish" is used, it is assumed that the General Assembly doesn't want a township to compose its own version. In effect, state statute says, "You can adopt regulations and standards that are in general use but you cannot make up your own."

The following townships have received voter approval for Limited Self-Government or Limited Home Rule:

Table 5-5: Township Limited Self-Government and Home Rule Voter Approval 1991-2001

County	Township	Est. 1999 Population*
Butler	Fairfield	14,899
Clermont	Miami	32,897
Hamilton	Delhi	30,291
Hamilton	Springfield	38,405
Hamilton	Sycamore	19,622
Hamilton	Symmes	14,445
Lucas	Sylvania	44,122
Mahoning	Boardman	41,708
Montgomery	Randolph	(now City of Clayton)
Montgomery	Washington	49,588
Stark	Jackson	34,268
Stark	Perry	31,750
Stark	Plain	51,883
Summit	Hudson	(now City of Hudson)
Trumbull	Howland	19,895
Warren	Hamilton	7,894

* The average estimated population of these townships is 30,833

Township Boundaries

The plan of government for the Northwest Territory called for state, county, and township governments. Municipal governments were not a part of that plan. Thus, on the level closest to the people, two

Township Government Today

kinds of government developed: one to be servant to the state, and the other to be servant to the people responsible for its creation (incorporation). Inevitably, conflict arose when the two local governments found themselves occupying the same ground. The issue: township boundaries. As a municipality increases in land area, the affected township often decreases in land area. This has given rise to traditional feuding between township and municipal interests. Statutes dealing with township boundaries are therefore a major factor in township-municipal relationships.

A considerable body of state law deals with township boundaries. Within each county, the county commission is designated as overseer of those laws. Commissioners make sure that procedures are followed and they approve or disapprove boundary changes.

Paper Townships

About half of the people in Ohio live in 1,309 functioning civil townships. Where do the other half live? Most people don't know it, but they live in 187 non-functioning townships. Non-functioning townships are called *paper townships* because they exist only on paper and perform no governmental functions. Residents of Akron, Cincinnati, and Toledo, for example, live in paper townships named Portage, Millcreek, and Adams.

Paper townships come about in two ways. First, a municipal government can separate itself from the township in which it is located. The municipal government can do this by creating a paper township inside its municipal borders. The effect of such an action is that the original township is reduced in size by loss of land area, and it no longer has any jurisdiction within the municipal limits. County commissioners *must* approve such a request by a city government and they *may* approve such a request from a village government. Second, when a municipal government expands to the point where it covers the entire land area of a civil township, the township "goes out of business" and becomes a paper township (or an addition to an existing paper township) inside the municipal boundaries.

There are 52 Ohio counties which have no paper townships and another 19 which have only one. Some counties contain many paper townships, ranging up to 57. For example, Lake County contains 13 paper townships; Summit county contains 17; Hamilton, 28; and Cuyahoga, 57. There are only two operating civil townships in Cuyahoga County.

> *Note:* Please see *Appendix B: The Annexation War of the Year 2000* following Chapter 8. Adoption of legislation constantly being brought before the General Assembly can modify what is written in this text about paper townships, withdrawal of municipal governments from townships, annexation, merger, and related municipal-township relationships.

Consolidation
Some municipalities occupy portions of two or more townships. The record was probably held by the City of Dublin which, in 1990, occupied portions of four civil townships. The number was reduced to three in 1991, two in 1995, and to one in 1997. This was accomplished by following a state law which allows municipal governments to ask that the land area of a township inside the municipality be annexed to the land area of another township inside the municipality. The 1991 action involved Washington Township in Franklin County and Concord Township in Delaware County. Concord territory was added to Washington Township. This was a precedent-setting action because it involved townships in two counties. The 1995 action involved Washington Township and Jerome Township in Union County. Jerome territory was added to Washington Township. The 1997 action added territory of Perry Township (Franklin County) to Washington Township. It is legally possible for Dublin to take further action to reduce the number of operating townships inside its city limits to zero. As with the creation of paper townships, requests by a city council to the county commission for consolidation of townships inside its city limits must be granted while such requests by village councils may be granted.

Township Government Today

Historically, townships were created first. When municipalities were established and when they expanded, municipal officials often decided to allow the civil townships to continue delivering whatever services they were delivering to the residents. Fire protection, for example, is commonly delivered by the township to municipal residents. However, the existence of a second or even a third township within the municipal limits can result in a wide disparity in the quality of some services received by the municipal residents. Thus, the municipal request to consolidate townships inside the municipality is taken to equalize the quality of services.

Once again: requests to alter township boundaries by city councils *must* be granted by the county commission while similar requests by village councils *may* be granted. This situation reflects the fact that the state constitution has established two classes of municipalities: cities and villages. The General Assembly can treat cities and villages differently so long as it treats all cities the same and all villages the same. We can only guess why the state law regarding changes to township boundaries was written as it is. Perhaps the General Assembly believed that village councils need assistance in determining what is in the best interest of the residents, both inside and outside the village.

Further Obligations of County Commissions
The regulation of township boundaries places further obligations on the county commission. The county commission is responsible for the following situations.

(1) Persons living outside a city or village can petition the county commission to redraw the township boundaries to exclude the portion of the township inside the municipality. Those people might think, for example, that they are subsidizing the cost of a service being extended to municipal residents. The commission is not obligated to grant the request, but it can decide the issue on merit. As with most rules, there is an exception to the rule that townships be everywhere. When township residents are successful in removing part of their township from a municipality, the portion of the municipality from which township area was removed is considered to be not in any township.

(2) Prior to 1999, any township that fell below 22 square miles in area had to be abolished and its land distributed to abutting townships. An exception was made for townships containing land inside a municipality. Another exception to the 22-square mile rule was enacted in 1999. That exception holds that with voter approval, a township operating under the Limited Home Rule form of government can remain in operation.

(3) Changes in township boundaries can require allocation of the affected township's debts and assets. If, for example, a township has debt and it loses half of its taxable property (tax base) due to a boundary change, the county commission might very well transfer half of the debt to the township or municipality which gained the taxable property.

(4) Finally, township property owners can request that radical surgery be performed on their township. They can ask, by petition: (a) that boundaries be changed by attaching a part of one township to another; (b) that a township be partitioned (divided into parts) and the parts be attached to other townships; and (c) that a new township be established from parts of existing townships. The county commission (or commissions) has the authority to grant such requests if it finds a good reason for doing so.

Township-Municipal Merger

If, by some magic, we could design and construct an ideal community in which to live, two basic ingredients would be home-rule powers and ample space for present and future development. Municipal governments can offer the strong home-rule powers. Most township governments can offer the space to grow. Once in a while, municipal and township officials decide to pool these assets in order to create the best possible community.

State law provides a two-step procedure whereby a township and a neighboring municipality can merge to form one municipality. First, state law requires the election of five people from each jurisdiction to form a ten-member merger commission. This is initiated by petition submitted to the County Board of Elections. The commission has about one year to study the pros and cons of merger and to prepare a report on the terms and conditions of merger. The report can deal with mutual concerns such as:

- representation on the village or city council,
- form of municipal government,
- taxes and debt,
- local laws to be enacted, amended, or repealed,
- will happen to employees, and
- what services will be provided by the new consolidated government.

Second, the citizens of both jurisdictions are allowed to vote on the terms and conditions of the merger. If approved in each jurisdiction, the two local governments become one. The following table illustrates the considerable interest shown in township-municipal merger during 1992–1999. The listing is of jurisdictions interested enough to study the feasibility of merger.

Table 5-6: Townships and Municipalities Willing to Consider Merger 1992-1999

County	Township	Municipality
Butler	Fairfield	Fairfield
Butler	Lemon	Monroe
Cuyahoga	Olmsted	Olmsted Falls
Fairfield	Greenfield	Carroll
Franklin	Plain	New Albany
Hamilton	Symmes	Montgomery
Hamilton	Symmes	Loveland
Licking	Etna	Kirkersville
Licking	Granville	Granville

Table 5-6 continued on next page

County	Township	Municipality
Licking	Lima*	Pataskala*
Licking	Union	Hebron
Montgomery	Randolph*	Clayton*
Montgomery	Madison*	Trotwood*
Ottawa	Danbury	Marblehead
Ottawa	Put in Bay	Put in Bay
Summit	Bath	Richfield
Summit	Boston	Peninsula
Summit	Franklin	Clinton
Summit	Hudson*	Hudson*
Summit	Richfield	Richfield
Summit	Twinsburg	Remindersville
Summit	Twinsburg	Twinsburg
Trumbull	Bazetta	Cortland
Warren	Deerfield	Mason

* Actual merger occurred

While the rate of township-municipal merger during 1992-1999 was under 20 percent, the significance here is that people are seeking or at least exploring a better future through cooperation. This is truly a grassroots effort of local officials because their state associations are not advocates of merger. Feasibility studies and voter information efforts are often conducted by amateurs. Ohio's newest township-municipal merged communities are: Randolph Township-Clayton, Madison Township-Trotwood, Lima Township-Pataskala, Hudson Township-Hudson. Earlier mergers include: Northhampton Township-Cuyahoga Falls, Green Township-Green, and Mad River Township-Riverside.

> **✓ Did you know?**
> Located in the state capitol city, the *Ohio Township Association* represents the interests of township government before the General Assembly and the departments of state government.
>
> Membership includes over 5,000 township trustees and clerks who serve in townships throughout the state. Members are organized both state-wide and by county.
>
> The Association publishes a bi-monthly magazine and sponsors state-wide and area-wide informational meetings for its members.
>
> Requests for information about township government in Ohio are welcome. Contact:
>
> Ohio Township Association
> 5969 E. Livingston Ave., Suite 110
> Columbus, Ohio 43232-2970
> Phone: (614) 863-0045
> Website: www.ohiotownships.org

Chapter 5 Review

■ Summary

At the close of the 20th century, there were 1,309 operating civil townships in Ohio. Roughly 75 percent have populations of less than 4,000. At the other end of the scale, 13 townships have populations of over 40,000. While no two townships are named alike in a single county, there are many with the same name throughout the state.

Today, township government has only four elected officials: three trustees and a clerk. Trustees have a dual policy-executive role. The clerk keeps financial and other records. Civil townships no longer have their own courts or handle poor relief, but the state legislature has granted, over a period of 150 years, the ability to provide or obtain many services for their residents. A variety of services for township residents can be provided by the township itself, by other local governments or private companies pursuant to contractual arrangements with the township government, or by special purpose districts. This has allowed township governments to cope with urbanization, but it can result in fragmented services to the residents.

Limited Self-Government, subject to voter approval, was granted to Ohio township governments in 1991. With Limited Self-Government, township trustees could enact laws to deal with minor crimes (misdemeanors) and impose fines. Limited Self-Government was expanded in 1999 and the name changed to Limited Home Rule. Additional powers were granted including the ability to carry out major public works projects and to assume additional debt.

Township boundaries are not permanent and boundary issues are settled by county commissions. Municipal governments can (1) request that there be no operating township within their borders, and can also (2) request that portions of two or more operating townships inside the municipality be consolidated. County commissions *must* grant such a request by a city and they *may* grant such a request from a village. There are additional circumstances which can lead to changes in township boundaries. Each case is decided by the county commission involved.

Merger is an option which is garnering increased attention. A township and a municipal government can combine into one unit of local government. It is a two-step procedure. First, voters in each jurisdiction elect five citizens to represent them on a merger commission. The commission prepares a report stating the terms and conditions of merger. That report is then accepted or rejected by the voters in both the township and the municipality.

Township Government Today

■ Glossary

Merge (Merger). The voluntary consolidation of a civil township and a municipality. Technically, merger is the annexation of a township to a municipality. It is also possible for two municipalities to merge.

Misdemeanor. A minor criminal offense. *Misdemeanor* includes traffic violations, petty theft, disorderly conduct, gambling, and other similar offenses. Misdemeanors are to be distinguished from felonies, which are more serious crimes.

Paper Township. A township in which all township offices have been abolished. Paper townships are located inside municipal borders.

Special District. A local government established to provide a single service. The service area can include one or more preexisting governments. Special districts can be used by pre-existing governments to bypass state-imposed taxing and debt limitations.

■ Review Questions

1. Are there more or less than 1,000 Ohio civil townships?
2. (True or false) Some Ohio townships have populations which are larger than the populations of some Ohio cities.
3. Are civil townships, or municipalities, or both, a part of the permanent organization of state government?
4. Do any Ohio townships have the same name?
5. Township government has how many elected officials? Name the offices.
6. A non-operating township located entirely inside municipal borders is called a _____ township.
7. Can all townships enact laws and impose fines for violators?
8. Can any Ohio township prohibit hunting or the sale or ownership of guns?
9. Can county commissioners refuse a request of a city to change township borders which intrude into the city?

10. The voluntary annexation or consolidation of a township with a municipality is called _____.

Answers to Review Questions: 1. More; 2. True; 3. Civil townships; 4. Yes; 5. Four. Three Trustees and a Clerk; 6. Paper; 7. No; 8. No; 9. No; 10. Merger.

Chapter 6: COUNTY GOVERNMENT

Introduction

The territorial policy of the Continental Congress was expressed in the Land Ordinance of 1785 and in the Northwest Ordinance of 1787. The 1785 law made land grants and sales feasible because specific places in the vast wilderness could be located. Land surveys were begun in 1786. The next order of business was to develop a plan of government for the lands northwest of the Ohio River, our first public domain. Plans were developed and set forth in the well-known Northwest Ordinance of 1787. The law, in fact, is so well known that it is often referred to simply as the Ordinance of 1787. It is famous because it set the precedent for how new land areas would be brought into the Union and how the residents would be treated prior to becoming citizens of the United States.

Politics, as the saying goes, is the art of compromise. Compromise surely took place when the members of the Continental Congress decided that local government in the Northwest Territory would consist of both counties and civil townships. Within the original 13 colonies (original states), *township government* was popular in the north while *county government* was popular in the south. Instead of choosing between the two, the Continental Congress decided to use both.

County government, as we shall discover in this chapter and the next, is something of a riddle. While it is structured to encourage inefficiency and it is highly resistant to change, it has great potential to bring greatly increased order and effectiveness to the entire field of local government in Ohio.

The Northwest Ordinance of 1787

"An Ordinance for the government of the United States northwest of the river Ohio." Thus reads the modest preamble to one of the most significant laws enacted by the Continental Congress. It is a bill of rights, a constitution, and a plan for territorial government. In it, individual and property rights are guaranteed. The Ordinance provides for, among other things, freedom of religion, trial by jury, support for schools, and the prohibition of slavery. It also assures settlers of inheritance rights—that is, the ability to pass on their property to their children and other descendants.

Government Structure of the Northwest Territory

Government of the Northwest Territory, as established by the Ordinance, was made up of a governor, a secretary, and three judges. The governor and secretary served in an executive capacity while the judges served in both a judicial and legislative capacity. Laws adopted and not vetoed by the governor were submitted to the Continental Congress for approval. The governor was also designated commander-in-chief of the militia. Those officials, who served until a general assembly (law-making body) was established, were appointed by the national Congress. A general assembly was to be elected when 5,000 males of voting age were living in the territory. When the population of an appropriate area reached 60,000, it became eligible for statehood.

Not less than three or more than five states were to be formed. Once formed, they would be admitted into the Union on an equal footing with the original 13 states. The governor was instructed to lay out, from time to time, counties and townships and to provide for their government. He also appointed local officials. The stated purpose of counties and townships was (1) to maintain law and order; and (2) to facilitate elections.

Creation of the Northwest Ordinance

The Ordinance of 1787 was adopted under unusual circumstances. Only 14 members of Congress were present when the vote was taken. The rest were in Philadelphia attending the Constitutional

Convention. However, a major business transaction would have been placed in jeopardy if action was delayed. An offer had been made to purchase 1,500,000 acres of the territory. Such a splendid opportunity to initiate the new territorial policy and to receive much-needed revenue at the same time could not be lost. Consequently, the Ohio Company of Associates, an organization of military veterans headed by General Rufus Putnam, obtained land located in and around what is now Marietta, Ohio. They paid about nine cents per acre. The settlement of the land northwest of the river Ohio had begun!

Arthur St. Clair

George Washington, Thomas Jefferson, and other members of the Continental Congress were the architects of government for the Northwest Territory. Their plans were set forth in the Northwest Ordinance of 1787. Arthur St. Clair, the first governor, was the builder. His building blocks were counties and their governments.

St. Clair's Early Life

In 1734, Arthur St. Clair was born into an aristocratic Scottish family. He was educated at the University of Edinburgh and briefly considered a career in medicine. Instead, at age 23, he joined the British army and received an ensign's commission. St. Clair was assigned to the Royal American Regiment, which may have been the same regiment in which Thomas Hutchins served (see Chapter 4). If so, St. Clair arrived in America when Hutchins was 28 years old and serving as quartermaster.

As a young aristocrat, Arthur St. Clair was well connected with many influential people. General Page, commandant of the British army in America was his cousin. At age 26, he received the rank of lieutenant and married the niece of Massachusetts Governor Bowdoin. St. Clair resigned his commission in 1762, after the close of the French and Indian War, to attend to the affairs of the Penn family which occupies a prominent place in the history of Pennsylvania.

St. Clair's Accomplishments in America

The American Revolution brought St. Clair back into the military, but this time on the side of the Americans. Congress quickly appointed him brigadier general, and then major general in 1777. As such, his troops fought along side those of General Washington throughout the American Revolution.

Figure 6-1: Arthur St. Clair

1787 was an important year for Arthur St. Clair. That year, St. Clair, the war hero, was elected to Congress and served as President of Congress. 1787 was also an important year for the country. The new United States Constitution was written, the

Northwest Ordinance was adopted, and settlement of the northwest began with the sale of land to the Ohio Company. Later that year, Arthur St. Clair received still another honor: he was appointed the first governor of the Northwest Territory.

A Turbulent Tenure as Governor

Governor St. Clair, at age 54, arrived in Marietta on July 15, 1788. His task was to conduct the first experiment of the United States Government in extending its original boundaries and authority. With the Ordinance of 1787 as a guide, he was to install law, order, and democracy throughout the territory. He would do this by establishing county and township governments which would eventually form the environment for state governments. Considering the vastness of the wilderness territory and with no precedent for guidance, the task was indeed difficult. It was made much more difficult by a major obstacle to settlement: Native Americans who resisted giving up their homelands.

Much of the land of the Northwest Territory was still claimed by the Native Americans. Here is what Article III, Section 14 of the Ordinance says on that subject:

> The utmost good faith shall always be observed towards the Indians; their lands and property shall never be taken from them without their consent; and in their property, rights, and liberty they shall never be invaded or disturbed, unless in just and lawful wars authorized by Congress; but laws founded in justice and humanity shall, from time to time, be made, for preventing wrongs being done to them, and for preserving peace and friendship with them.

Realizing the need for understanding with the native tribes, St. Clair devoted a great deal of time seeking treaties. A central point of such treaties specified where the tribe relinquished land for settlement by the newcomers. While some tribes were willing to negotiate, two were not. The Shawnee and Miamis insisted that the Ohio River forever separate Native Americans from what they considered to be invaders. In response to attacks on settlers north of the Ohio River, a punitive expedition was sent against the Miamis in 1790 with disastrous results for both sides. After burning six villages near what is now Fort Wayne, Indiana, and destroying the winter food supply, the withdrawing American army was attacked and nearly 200 soldiers were killed.

The battle prompted a letter from President Washington to Governor St. Clair. Based on friendship, respect, and experience, Washington stated, he would once again appoint St. Clair as major general and give him responsibility for military operations in the Northwest Territory. Within six months, a new army was formed and St. Clair set off with about 3,000 troops to establish fortifications intended to contain the Native Americans.

The Shawnees and Miamis attacked St. Clair's troops on November 3, 1791 near the present-day boundary between Ohio and Indiana. The results were devastating. Never during the frontier Indian wars was an American army more soundly defeated. The assault led by Miami Chief Little Turtle and Shawnee Chief Blue Jacket took place in what is now Mercer County, Ohio. 630 soldiers were killed; 238 were wounded. This eclipses the famous "Custer's Last Stand" during which 264 soldiers were killed on June 25, 1876. Although St. Clair was not held responsible for the defeat, he resigned as commander of the army. However, he continued to serve as governor for 11 more years.

St. Clair Opposes Ohio Statehood
When the number of male settlers in the territory reached 5,000 in the year 1799, a General Assembly was elected. The Assembly served as a legislative branch of government, which marked the beginning of the end to St. Clair's one-man rule. During his tenure as governor, he was able to create counties and their governments, wage wars, and help establish law and order. In the end, however, he was not able to cope with the politics of statehood for Ohio. One political party, the Federalists, was against statehood while the other political party, the Republicans, favored it. Thomas Jefferson, a Republican, wanted more Republican members of Congress, and when St. Clair opposed Ohio statehood in 1802, he was fired. He returned to his home in Pennsylvania where he died in the year

1818.

The First Counties

St. Clair's first official act upon arriving in Marietta was to create Washington County. As originally established, it was almost half the size in area of present day Ohio. Most of the counties established prior to statehood were very large in area compared to counties today. Below is a list of counties established during St. Clair's tenure.

Table 6-1: The First Counties

Ohio Counties	Creation Date
Washington	1788
Hamilton	1790
Jefferson	1791
Adams	1797
Ross	1798
Belmont	1800
Clermont	1800
Fairfield	1800
Trumbull	1800

After Ohio became a state, counties were created by the Ohio General Assembly. The work of the territorial government was continued by the General Assembly without any abrupt changes in policies or procedures. In 1803, eight new counties were formed: Butler, Greene, Columbiana, Franklin, Montgomery, Scioto, Gallia, and Warren.

Figure 6-2: County Boundaries in 1797 and 1803
Ohio Counties in 1797, Arthur St. Clair's 9th year as governor

Ohio counties in 1803, when Ohio achieved statehood

County Government 103

Figure 6-3: Ohio Counties Today

The rest of Ohio's 88 counties were formed after 1803. Although the last county, Noble County, was formed in 1851, boundary changes and adjustments continued until 1888.

Ohio's counties are small when compared to those of other states. Ohio counties average 470 square miles in size. The national average is 600 square miles. Ohio counties, like townships, were laid out to meet the requirements of farm life in the 19th century.

County Government Structure

The duties assigned to county government by the state government change from time to time. Those duties, however, are performed by governmental machinery which was designed for the 19th century.

An Executive Branch with Many Twigs

The big difference between county government and other governments is the way the executive branch of county government is organized, or to put it in a better way, is disorganized. County government has 11 elected officials. There are three commissioners and one of each of the following: auditor, clerk of courts, coroner, engineer, prosecuting attorney, recorder, sheriff, and treasurer. Each performs the duties to which he or she is elected. The result is that county government has many independent executive branches. Perhaps each can be called an *executive twig*. Each executive twig has its own elected person or persons in charge, and there is no single chief executive like a president or governor to manage the entire branch. Without a chief executive, responsibility for doing a good job is scattered throughout the county government. Good management requires that responsibility be centralized.

The Elected County Officials

Article X, Section 1 of the Ohio Constitution states, in part, that the General Assembly shall provide by general law for the organization and government of counties. No county office is established in the Constitution. The offices of all elected officials are established by legislative act as are the duties of the various officials. Thus, county offices can be changed or abolished by a vote of the General Assembly or by initiative of the people; no constitutional amendment is required.

Most of the elected county offices go a long way back into American and British history. For example, no county office has a longer or more colorful past than that of sheriff. Those who have read the novel, *Robin Hood*, by Paul Creswick, know that the Sheriff of Nottingham was a powerful man. Back in the days of Robin Hood, about 800 years ago, the sheriff of a British shire (county) was the king's representative and lived in a castle. Acting in the name of the king, the sheriff's authority was extensive. Today, Ohio's county officials perform duties assigned or allowed not by a king but instead by the Ohio General Assembly. Some of the major duties performed by the elected county officials are described in the following paragraphs.

Sheriff
The U.S. Congress, in 1792, authorized the sheriff's position for county government within the Northwest Territory. The law enforcement duties have not changed very much since then. The sheriff can still form a posse to pursue and capture criminals; however, he can no longer hang them. His responsibility to serve as executioner was taken away in 1866.

The sheriff is the county's chief law enforcement officer. In addition to law enforcement, today's sheriffs operate county jails and are "servants of the court." That means that they perform tasks such as delivering legal papers.

Coroner
In 1788, the coroner position was authorized for the Northwest Territory. The coroner and sheriff positions always have been closely related. The county coroner investigates suspicious deaths, violent deaths, and the deaths of persons who die in prison. Since 1945, coroners and assistant coroners must be registered physicians (medical doctors).

Clerk of Courts
The clerk of courts position has a history dating back to 13th century England. The clerk maintains the records of both the court of common pleas and the court of appeals. The clerks in some counties also perform duties for municipal or county court. Other records, in addition to those of the courts, are filed with the clerk. Included in this category are those of the county coroner. The clerk of courts is also responsible for issuing titles for motor vehicles and watercraft.

Prosecuting Attorney
This is a relatively new position which did not exist during territorial days. After Ohio became a state, the court of common pleas was authorized to appoint an attorney to act on behalf of the county government. The attorney's job was to prepare cases to be tried by the court and to prosecute those cases. In the year 1833, the elected office of prosecuting attorney was established. In addition to the court-related work, the office holder gives legal advice to county and township officials. The prosecuting attorney is also legal adviser for public libraries and public school districts except city school districts. The attorney employed by the city in which the city school district is located serves as legal advisor to the city school district.

Recorder
In 1795, the Congress authorized the office of recorder in the Northwest Territory. The recorder keeps track of land transactions (the buying and selling of land). Chapter 4 describes the surveys and other steps taken by the national government to dispose of the wilderness lands by sale or grant. The recorder position was established as a part of that effort.

Today, the county recorder still keeps records dealing with land ownership. For any lot or parcel of land in the county, the records of the county recorder will show who owns it and whether someone is buying or leasing it. The county recorder also records subdivision plats, all county and township zoning regulations and amendments, and other legal documents.

Surveyor/Engineer
The early settlers had to find their land, which was no easy task. The county surveyor position was created to help people locate their land. Over the years, the county surveyors became more and more involved in the construction and maintenance of county-owned roads, buildings, and other facilities. In 1935, the name of the position was changed to county engineer. Today, the primary duty of the county engineer is to plan, design, construct, and maintain the

county road system including county bridges. The engineer also has responsibility for township bridges and for bridges on certain through routes inside municipalities. He or she also provides engineering services for the townships.

Auditor and Treasurer

These two separately elected positions have one common interest: money. The treasurer is the county's banker. The office has custody of the county's money from the time it is collected until it is spent. The auditor, on the other hand, is the chief fiscal officer of the county. He or she keeps track of the money due and authorizes expenditures.

One major task performed by the auditor's office is the administration of Ohio's property tax laws. This involves the appraisal for tax purposes of all properties in the county. After the property taxes are collected by the treasurer, the auditor distributes the money back to the local governments which levied the property taxes.

Board of County Commissioners: The Governing Body

County commissions are newcomers to Ohio local government. They did not exist during territorial days. Instead, each county had what was known as a *Court of General Quarter Sessions*. Three or more justices of the peace (minor judges) met quarterly to handle the business of the county government. Those men were appointed by Governor St. Clair. Business included such matters as creating civil townships, adopting a budget, paying bills, appointing tax collectors, and contracting for road work.

Today, except for Summit County, counties have three-member commissions. The charter of Summit County provides for a seven-member council. Whether it is called a commission or a council, however, it is the closest thing there is to a governing body. The term *governing body* is not exactly accurate because a county commission has very limited control over the other elected county officials.

> ### ✓ Did you know?
> The *County Commissioners Association of Ohio* (CCAO) is the oldest organization of its kind in the United States. Formed in 1880, CCAO has served as an organization to improve county government for over 120 years.
>
> CCAO promotes effective county government operations, represents county government interests before the General Assembly and state agencies, and provides reference and research services. The Association holds state-wide meetings and conferences and publishes a magazine, as well as other informational materials.
>
> Inquiries concerning Ohio county government are welcome. Contact:
>
> County Commissioners Association of Ohio
> 37 West Broad Street, Suite 650
> Columbus, Ohio 43215
> Phone: (614) 221-5627   Website: www.ccao.org
>
> Some associations of county officials do not have permanent addresses. However, CCAO can help you to contact:
> - The County Auditors Association of Ohio
> - County Clerk of Courts Association of Ohio
> - Ohio State County Coroners Association of Ohio
> - County Prosecutors Association of Ohio
> - County Treasurers Association of Ohio
> - Buckeye State Sheriffs Association
> - County Recorders Association of Ohio
> - County Engineers Association of Ohio

Many additional tasks have been assigned to county government since Ohio became a state. Unless they were clearly related to one of the other elected offices, those new tasks became the responsibility of the board of county commissioners. The county commissions are responsible for many very important services. A partial listing includes aid to the poor and handicapped, public health, trash disposal, and the care of county-owned buildings.

County Government

Figure 6-4: Franklin County Organizational Chart

Elected Offices

County Commissioners	Auditor
Coroner	Engineer
Prosecutor	Sheriff
Treasurer	Clerk of Courts
Appeals Court Judge	Common Pleas Court Judge
Domestic Relations Court Judge	Probate Court Judge

Departments of the County Commission

Office on Aging	Animal Control
Child Support Enforcement	Fleet Management
Human Services	Public Facilities Management
Purchasing	Sanitary Engineer
Building Regulation and Zoning	

County Agencies
(Semi-independent)

Alcohol Drug Addiction and Mental Health Services Board	Alliance for Cooperative Justice
Children Services	Educational Services Center
Board of Elections	Board of Health
Emergency Management Agency	Mental Retardation / Developmental Disabilities
Metropolitan Parks	Planning Commission
Parks and Recreation Columbus Baseball Team	Rickenbacker Port Authority
Solid Waste Management Authority	Soil & Water Conservation District
Veterans Service Commission	Public Defender

County commissioners also deal extensively with other local governments. For example, they decide municipal annexation (growth in land area) issues and, as indicated in Chapter 5, they can change civil township boundaries. In both instances, county commissions hold public hearings during which municipal and township officials present their case. The issue is settled by vote of the commissioners.

The commissioners are expected to coordinate the activities of the other elected county officials. The commission is the general administrative body of the county government. It is the taxing, budgeting and purchasing authority and holds title to all county-owned property. In addition, the county commission receives annual reports from the sheriff, engineer, treasurer, clerk of courts, and the prosecuting attorney.

Term of Office and Salary
County officials are elected for four-year terms in even-numbered years. All county officials except one commissioner and the auditor are elected during one election. Then, one commissioner and the auditor are elected two years later. Salaries are set by the General Assembly based on county population. Officials of counties with large populations are paid more than officials of counties with small populations. Elected officials are not obligated to work any specific number of hours per day or per week; they are simply expected to carry out the duties of their office.

The Judicial Branch
The term *county courthouse* has always been synonymous with county government. A basic function of county government has been to establish and to maintain law and order. Within each county courthouse is a court of common pleas which has the following types of jurisdiction: (1) appellate jurisdiction from decisions of the board of county commissioners, (2) original jurisdiction for all criminal cases except for minor offenses which can be heard by an inferior court, and (3) original jurisdiction in all civil cases where the sum in dispute exceeds that which can be handled by an inferior court. Decisions of the court of common pleas can be appealed to the court of appeals and finally to the Ohio Supreme Court. Courts inferior to the court of common pleas are municipal courts and county courts.

Figure 6-5: The Ohio Court System

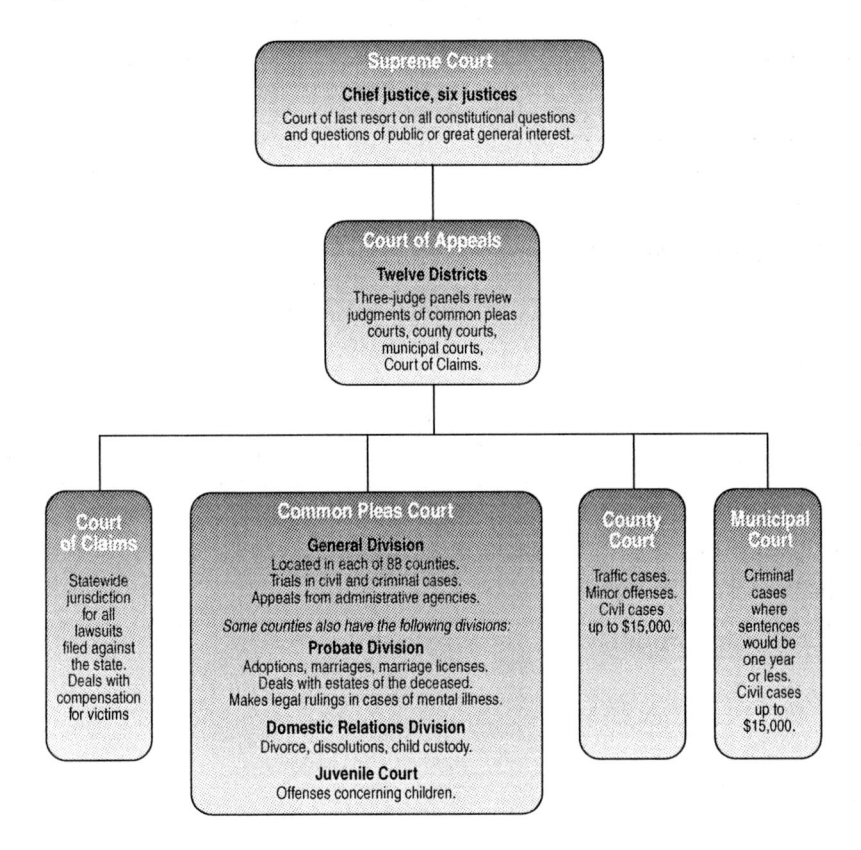

Supreme Court
Chief justice, six justices
Court of last resort on all constitutional questions and questions of public or great general interest.

Court of Appeals
Twelve Districts
Three-judge panels review judgments of common pleas courts, county courts, municipal courts, Court of Claims.

Court of Claims
Statewide jurisdiction for all lawsuits filed against the state. Deals with compensation for victims.

Common Pleas Court
General Division
Located in each of 88 counties.
Trials in civil and criminal cases.
Appeals from administrative agencies.

Some counties also have the following divisions:
Probate Division
Adoptions, marriages, marriage licenses.
Deals with estates of the deceased.
Makes legal rulings in cases of mental illness.

Domestic Relations Division
Divorce, dissolutions, child custody.

Juvenile Court
Offenses concerning children.

County Court
Traffic cases. Minor offenses. Civil cases up to $15,000.

Municipal Court
Criminal cases where sentences would be one year or less. Civil cases up to $15,000.

The judicial branch of county government is independent. The primary and paramount purpose of a courthouse is to furnish the rooms and facilities essential for the proper and efficient performance of the court. Although the board of county commissioners has full control over office space provided by them for use by other county officers, the judiciary assumes full control over a building – or part thereof – assigned to it. The board of county commissioners has little or no discretion over the judicial budget.

County governments pay all or some of the costs of the lower courts. The lower courts include the county court, the municipal court, and the court of common pleas. Often, a municipality and a county will share the cost of maintaining a municipal court when jurisdiction extends beyond the municipal limits.

Chapter 6 Review

■ Summary

The Northwest Ordinance, also called the Ordinance of 1787, was the plan of government for territory acquired from the British at the close of the Revolutionary War. It established the important policy that new territories were to be developed for admission to statehood on an equal footing with all other states. There were to be no fewer than three nor more than five states formed from the Northwest Territory.

A temporary territorial government was established. Offices (a governor, secretary, and three judges) were filled by Congressional appointment. The duties of the governor and secretary were executive in nature while the duties of the three judges were both legislative and judicial in nature. A major responsibility of the temporary government was to establish a governmental framework consisting of counties and townships. A general assembly (legislative body) was to be elected when there were 5,000 males of voting age in the territory. When the population reached 60,000, the territory would be eligible for statehood.

Arthur St. Clair was the first governor of the Northwest Territory and he served until 1802. He was a strong-willed person with powers to match his personality. During his tenure he was able to create local governments, appoint local officials, and veto legislation enacted in the territory. He was able to wage war and help bring law and order to the wilderness. St. Clair, however, was not able to cope with the politics of statehood. He was fired by President Thomas Jefferson because he opposed statehood for the Ohio Territory. St. Clair did not believe that the settlers were ready for such a responsibility.

Washington County was the first county created in what is now

County Government

Ohio. In all, nine counties were created prior to statehood. After Ohio became a state, the task of forming counties was assumed by the Ohio General Assembly. There have been no changes to county boundaries since 1888. Ohio's counties are small when compared to those of other states. Ohio counties average 440 square miles in size while the national average is 600 square miles.

County government in Ohio does not have a chief executive officer. Overall responsibility for county government is not centralized in any one office. The county executive branch has many "twigs" of government. This awkward organization of county government has been established by state statute (that is, by the General Assembly). Change can be made by the General Assembly or by the people through the use of an initiative petition. No constitutional amendments are necessary.

Many of the elected county executive offices have long and colorful histories. They include sheriff, coroner, clerk of courts, recorder, engineer (or surveyor), auditor, and treasurer. The prosecuting attorney and county commissioner are elected executive offices which have been created since statehood.

The county commission is the nearest thing there is to a governing body. It has limited authority over the other elected officials, but it does levy all county taxes and it budgets for all county offices. It also purchases for all county offices and it holds title to all county property.

■ Glossary

Federalists. The first American political party. It evolved during the last years of George Washington's presidency and advocated a strong central government.

Militia. The volunteer armed forces of the states. Part-time citizen soldiers.

Public domain. Public lands owned by the United States government. Territorial lands have been sold or given away in the form of land grants. However, national parks and forests, Indian reservations, grazing districts, and miscellaneous holdings remain.

Republican. (As that term applies to Jefferson) Thomas Jefferson's political party had the name *Democrat-Republican*. The party advocated strong states and a minimal national government. It placed major emphasis on individual freedom and responsibility.

■ Review Questions

1. What law enacted by the Continental Congress established the principle that new states would be equal in legal stature to the original 13 states?
2. (True or false) The required structure of government within the Northwest Territory consisted of states, counties, and townships.
3. (True or false) The Ordinance of 1787 required that cities and towns be established in strategic locations throughout the Northwest Territory.
4. Who was the first governor of the Northwest Territory and what governing body appointed him?
5. What was the first county created in the Northwest Territory?
6. In today's county government, are executive (management) responsibilities centralized or scattered throughout the organization?
7. In county government, what is the nearest thing to a governing body?
8. What county office investigates suspicious deaths?
9. What county office collects property taxes?
10. Questions concerning the valuation of buildings for property tax purposes should be directed to what county office?

Answers to Review Questions: 1. The Northwest Ordinance, also called the Ordinance of 1787; 2. True; 3. False; 4. Arthur St. Clair, appointed by the Continental Congress; 5. Washington; 6. Scattered; 7. The county commission; 8. Coroner; 9. Treasurer; 10. Auditor.

Chapter 7: COUNTY HOME RULE

In 1902, Professor Martin Andrews of Marietta College wrote, "In the civil history of the county, there is little that is exciting or curious." This is perhaps still true. Occasionally, however, events and people conspire to make change. Such an occurrence took place in 1933 when the state constitution was amended to allow county home rule.

The Cincinnati Reform Movement

The drive for county home rule was a consequence of municipal reform. The dawn of the 20th century found chaotic conditions in many American cities. Mutual distrust, fed by economic and social disparities, separated political, labor, religious, and immigrant groups from one another and from the upper class citizenry. Living conditions for the masses were all too often crowded, unsanitary, and lawless. A Cincinnati newspaper reported that Sundays in the inner city were "a carnival of drunkenness, base sensuality, reeking debauchery and bloody, often fatal, crimes." Such conditions resulted in overwhelming demands on city governments for more and better services. Many, especially the largest cities, could not meet that challenge. The resulting breakdown of municipal government allowed the rise of the *political boss.*

A political boss is a politician who controls a state or local party organization primarily for personal gain, not to benefit the public. Although much has been written about the unethical conduct of political bosses, two positive events took place during their era:

(1) political bosses took control and were able to produce results when others were paralyzed by the problems of urbanization, and (2) the era of the political boss ushered in the era of political reform. The primary power of the political boss was the ability to get candidates nominated and elected to public office. Once elected, those office holders owed favors.

Cincinnati's Boss Cox
One of the most colorful political bosses was George Barnesdale Cox, better known as "Boss Cox." He influenced, and in many ways, controlled the political affairs of Cincinnati and Hamilton County for roughly a quarter of a century. Because political bosses were not elected or appointed, it is not possible to know exactly when they came into power. In Cox's case, it is reasonable to assume the late-1880s. By way of introduction, we can consider his comments made during an interview by a newspaper reporter. When asked for the reasons for his success in his chosen occupation, Cox replied, "I never violated a pledge in my life and I never supported a man without being asked to do so. I probably made enemies along the way but if I didn't, I would have no friends." He went on to state his belief that, "the man who makes possible the nomination should be first considered when favors are passed around."

Those favors included the ability to place people in government jobs and to direct purchasing and construction contracts to his friends and family members. (For example, he managed to have his brother appointed as purchasing agent for the City of Cincinnati.) For many years, Cox himself was on the payroll of the local natural gas company. He saw no difference between his relationship with the company and that of a lawyer or lobbyist working on behalf of the company.

The handing out of government jobs to political helpers is known as the *spoils system*. The name is probably based on the old adage, "To the victor belongs the spoils." During the age of boss rule, on all levels of government, election victory meant that people employed by the opposition party would be replaced. This was known as the post-election *clean sweep*. Little or no attention was given to qualifications; party loyalty was the only requirement.

Figure 7-1: Boss Cox
A newspaper reporter described Cox as being six feet tall, weighing 200 pounds, and looking very much like an ordinary businessman.

Cox started his political career as a worker for the Republican Party in Ward 18 of the City of Cincinnati. He soon rose to ward captain and subsequently advanced into more influential circles and party leadership roles. During his career, he managed not only local politicians, but also campaigns for state and national offices. Cox was usually able to deliver Hamilton County for the politicians he supported. Although he wielded a great deal of power, Cox himself was elected to only one public office: he served two terms on city council.

Democratic victories in 1911 and charges of corruption encouraged a wing of the Republican Party to revolt against Cox. His 25-year reign was not overthrown completely, but it steadily weakened from that year on. Reformers (both political parties and civic groups) became more active in their effort to improve the city government. A new coalition of civic activists formed an organization which they called the Charter Party. They designed a modern government for Cincinnati and, in 1926, successfully won adoption of a new municipal charter. The Council-Manager form of government was selected and Cincinnati soon became one of the best-governed cities in the United States.

On to the County!
If the quality of city government could be improved by citizen action, why not the county? The Cincinnati reform movement spilled out beyond the city limits under the direction of the Citizens Committee, a group which had been active in civic affairs for many years. In 1933, the Cincinnati reformers teamed up with other reform groups throughout Ohio and successfully submitted, by petition, an amendment to Article 10 of the state constitution. Here is how the issue was worded on the state-wide ballot:

> The amendment proposes to provide for the organization and government of counties. It authorizes any county to frame, adopt or amend a charter and establish a form of government; permits the legislature to enact plans of government subject to adoption by the electors of any county; provides for the transfer of powers of townships

and municipalities to the county, or for the withdrawal of such powers by a vote of the people concerned; permits the adoption of a charter giving the county concurrent or exclusive municipal powers, or making the county a consolidated municipality; provides for the choosing of a charter commission by popular vote and for the framing of a charter by such commission. *Summarizing, it provides a form of "County Home Rule Government."* (emphasis added)

This revolutionary amendment deals with much more than county government. In effect, it tells the people that they can determine the roles that township, municipal, and county governments will play within the area of their own county. For example, citizens can change the organization of their county government by consolidating county functions and expanding the role of the county commission. Some or all or the elected independent offices (that is, auditor, clerk of courts, coroner, engineer, prosecuting attorney, recorder, sheriff, and treasurer) can be consolidated and/or eliminated. A chief executive can be elected by the people or appointed by the commission.

Perhaps the most amazing aspect of the County Home Rule Amendment is that it grants authority to the people to transfer powers from the township and municipal governments to the county. Voters can even turn the county into a consolidated municipality. In other words, the whole county can become a city-county which performs both county and municipal functions. Under this example, which is admittedly extreme, existing municipal and township governments would vanish. Thus, the people of Ohio have the ability to keep their current system of government, create consolidated city-counties, or invent something in between.

Change has been an elusive goal. The County Home Rule Amendment was adopted in 1933. Since then, there have been 33 county home rule issues on the ballots of 11 counties. The result: one home rule charter has been adopted.

Charter Commissions

Reform groups, located throughout the state, greeted the home rule amendment with enthusiasm. In 1934, charter commissions were requested in eight counties. A *charter commission* is created to draft or design a charter, a document that defines how the government is organized. (For more information on charters, See Chapter 2.) Voters approved the formation of commissions in Cuyahoga, Hamilton, Lucas, and Mahoning Counties. They rejected the formation of commissions for Franklin, Montgomery, Stark, and Summit Counties.

A county charter commission is created only after receiving approval from the voters. The question, "Shall a county charter commission be chosen?" will be placed on the ballot if: (1) the county commission receives a petition signed by eight percent of the eligible voters asking that the question be placed on the ballot, or (2) the county commission itself places the question on the ballot. In either event, the process requires two elections. First, voters are asked to approve the establishment of a charter commission and to elect 15 members to serve on the commission. The charter commission must then design the new county government, draft a proposed charter, and inform the residents of their decisions. Second, the voters are asked to approve the proposed charter. The whole process must take place within one year. For example, formation of a charter commission might be approved during a general election (November) and then the commission's proposed charter will be voted on during the next general election.

Since 1934, the question of forming a charter commission has been posed at least another eight times. Cuyahoga County received approval to form a charter commission in 1949, and again in 1958. Lucas County received approval in 1958, and Montgomery County in 1961. Summit County received permission in 1969 and again in 1974. Lake County got the okay in 1970, as did Trumbull County in 1972. Overall, since 1933 when the Ohio Constitution was amended to allow it, the creation of at least 12 charter commissions have been approved and four have been disapproved. The numbers used here are qualified with "at least" because the historical record is far from clear.

At least 11 county charters have been drafted by elected charter commissions and *every one of them have been rejected at the polls*. (Remember that charter approval is a two-step process.) Proposed charters have, for example, provided for organizational consolidation, wider representation, a chief executive officer, the elimination of some of the elected independent offices, and even the assumption of some municipal powers.

Charters By Petition

The road leading to adoption of a county charter is filled with obstacles. Opponents can wage a campaign to defeat the establishment of a charter commission. That can stop the process at the very beginning. Opponents can also run as candidates to serve on the commission. If elected, they can do their best to preserve the current system of government (the *status quo*). Some obstacles were removed in 1978 when Article 10 of the constitution was amended to provide another avenue by which a proposed charter can be developed and brought to a vote of the people. The 1978 amendment provides that a proposed charter drafted by any person or persons can be placed on the ballot. A petition signed by ten percent of the registered voters is required. When the petition and draft charter are received by the county commission, the issue must be certified to the board of elections to be placed on the ballot.

This new route was followed by Summit County in 1979. Here something different happened: the Summit County charter was approved! The petition route was followed by Cuyahoga County in 1980, and again in 1989, and by Columbiana County in both 1989 and 1990. A 1998 effort by Hamilton County sports enthusiasts was more concerned with the location of a baseball stadium than with the county government. The proposed Hamilton County charter fixed the location of the new Cincinnati Reds stadium while leaving the county government basically unchanged. To the relief of many students of good government, the proposed Hamilton County charter was defeated at the polls. A charter should deal only with the internal workings of government.

Table 7-1: Chronological Record of Attempts to Establish County Home Rule

County	Year	Question	Result
Cuyahoga	1934	Elect Commission?	Yes
Franklin	1934	Elect Commission?	No
Hamilton	1934	Elect Commission?	Yes
Lucas	1934	Elect Commission?	Yes
Mahoning	1934	Elect Commission?	Yes
Montgomery	1934	Elect Commission?	No
Stark	1934	Elect Commission?	No
Summit	1934	Elect Commission?	No
Cuyahoga	1935	Adopt charter?	No
Hamilton	1935	Adopt charter?	No
Lucas	1935	Adopt charter?	No
Mahoning	1935	Adopt charter?	No
Cuyahoga	1949	Elect Commission?	Yes
Cuyahoga	1950	Adopt charter?	No
Cuyahoga	1958	Elect Commission?	Yes
Lucas	1958	Elect Commission?	Yes
Cuyahoga	1959	Adopt charter?	No
Lucas	1959	Adopt charter?	No
Montgomery	1961	Elect Commission?	Yes
Summit	1969	Elect Commission?	Yes
Summit	1970	Approve charter?	No
Lake	1970	Elect Commission?	Yes
Lake	1971	Approve charter?	No
Trumbull	1972	Elect Commission?	Yes

Trumbull	1973	Approve charter?	No
Summit	1974	Elect Commission?	Yes
Summit	1975	Approve charter?	No
Summit	1979*	Approve charter?	Yes
Cuyahoga	1980*	Approve charter?	No
Cuyahoga	1989*	Approve charter?	No
Columbiana	1989*	Approve charter?	No
Columbiana	1990*	Approve charter?	No
Hamilton	1998*	Approve charter?	No

* Denotes attempts by petition.

The Summit County Charter

When analyzed, the Summit County charter appears timid in its approach to reform. That charter is the least disruptive to the traditional organization of county government and to the role of the political parties. The Summit County charter appears timid, that is, until it is remembered that it was approved on the fourth try. Efforts had been defeated at the polls in 1934 to elect a commission and in both 1970 and 1975 to approve charters developed by commissions.

As approved, the charter provides for an elected county executive and an 11-member county council. This is rather like a municipal mayor and council. The charter has survived amendments including one which eliminated the office of Recorder and another which modified the office of Coroner. The position title is now Medical Examiner and the office holder is appointed by and responsible to the county executive.

Opposition to Change

Why do the voters keep rejecting proposed county charters? Some probable causes are:

(1) Voter apathy and a lack of knowledge concerning county government;

(2) Opposition from the elected independent office holders and from those who wish to take their place; and

(3) With rare exception, opposition from political parties because county government (a) offers a reservoir of patronage offices and jobs and; (b) is the conduit to the well known "grass roots" from which each political party claims to spring.

Patronage

Patronage is the right to control the distribution of jobs in the public service. The concept of patronage is a throw-back to the old "spoils system" mentioned earlier in the chapter (although certainly the post-election "clean sweep" is no longer possible). Today, many government entities choose employees through the *Civil Service System*. Civil Service is a personnel system designed to recruit and retain qualified government employees. Even where Civil Service has replaced the old spoils system, political parties still select and support candidates, and there are appointed jobs at all levels of government which are exempt from Civil Service.

The Grass Roots Connection

In order to be truly effective, a political party must function on all three levels of government (national, state and local). A politician can begin his or her political career on the local level, advance to the state level, and go on to the national level. This leads to another reason for political parties to shun county home rule government: county charter commissions usually substitute appointed positions for elected positions. This can cause concern among the parties. As the number of elected positions declines, so too does the relevance of political parties.

Four Hurdles

The largest obstacle to change by charter, however, is within Article 10 itself. A proposed charter which bestows any "municipal" powers must be approved by the voters in four ways, the so-called *four hurdles*. A charter which confers municipal powers must be approved by a majority of voters: (1) in the county, (2) living outside the largest city, (3) living inside the largest city, and (4) in each of a majority of the combined total of municipalities and townships. In other words, a proposed county charter which bestows any "municipal" powers must be approved in so many ways that its adoption is extremely doubtful. The fourth requirement was dropped for counties with populations of 500,000 or more by a 1957 amendment to Article 10. This includes Cuyahoga, Franklin, Hamilton, Montgomery, and Summit Counties.

The Cuyahoga County Experience

Four proposed Cuyahoga County charters have been defeated at the polls. Elections in 1935, 1950, and 1959 resulted in defeat of charters developed by commissions. The charter defeated in 1980 was submitted to the voters by petition. The 1935 attempt was the most noteworthy of the four.

In 1935, several reform groups, including the League of Women Voters and the Civic League, advocated metropolitan government. These reformers believed that a central government with county-wide ability to handle both urban and rural situations would be more effective than a multitude of separate jurisdictions. However, many people from the suburbs of Cleveland opposed the idea. Fearing a new "super government" controlled by Cleveland political interests, they formed the Suburban Charter League to oppose the reform groups. During the struggle, some suburbs threatened to secede from Cuyahoga County if a charter granting broad powers to the county was adopted. (The threat was made despite the fact there is no provision under Ohio law to do so.)

Fortunately, there were moderates on the 1935 charter commission, which was headed by Harold H. Burton, a popular candidate for Cleveland Mayor. The moderates opted for what they claimed was a simple reorganization of the county government. The proposed charter provided for a chief executive appointed by a nine-member legislative body. The existing county offices (auditor, treasurer, and so on) would be headed by appointees of the chief executive.

Burton promoted the adoption of the county home rule charter as a cost cutting measure, which, in turn, helped promote his candidacy for mayor. The people of Cleveland gave election victories to both Burton and the proposed charter. The charter also won on a county-wide basis. It appeared the reformers had won on the first try! The board of elections, however, refused to recognize the victory. The board believed that all four hurdles, not just two, had to be cleared. The state supreme court was asked to settle the dispute. The court ruled in 1936 that the charter was not merely a simple reorganization, but a grant of municipal powers to the county. Therefore, the issue failed because it did not clear all four hurdles.

What is a Municipal Power?

A *municipal power*, according to the 1936 decision, is simply a power possessed by municipal governments. The court reviewed the charter to determine whether it allowed Cuyahoga County to do things that, in Ohio, a municipal government can do, but a regular county government can't do. Three such powers were identified.

(1) *The power to legislate.* The charter provided for the enactment of ordinances by the legislative body and it also allowed legislation by the people (the initiative and referendum).

(2) *The power to enforce municipal ordinances.* The sheriff's position was replaced by a director of public safety who was empowered to enforce not only state and county statutes but also laws passed by city and village councils. Other Ohio counties have no authority to enforce municipal ordinances.

(3) *The power to adopt a Civil Service personnel system.* In 1936, Civil Service was practiced by cities but not by counties.

Cuyahoga County Today

The visions of the 1930s reform groups did not materialize. Instead of one unified government providing basic services on a county-wide basis, there exist 38 cities, 19 villages, two operating townships, and the county government. Added to this are numerous special districts—metropolitan or area-wide agencies formed to provide specific public services. These are the inconspicuous governments managed by professionals who are relatively unknown to the general public. Inconspicuous governments are responsible for, among other things, metropolitan parks, the metropolitan hospital system, metropolitan sewer service, metropolitan housing authority, and metropolitan regional transit.

Alternative Forms of Government

The County Home Rule Amendment, adopted in 1933, not only allows charter government, but also provides that the General Assembly may provide, by general law, alternative forms of county government. Twenty-eight years later, in 1961, the General Assembly created two alternative plans of county government. The first alternative form provides for an elected county executive with duties similar to those of a city mayor. The second provides for a less independent county executive appointed by and subject to the direction of the county commission. The position is roughly comparable to that of a city manager.

The number of county commissioners can be increased. The greatest power granted to the county commissioners under both alternative forms of county government is that of the home rule or limited legislative powers. The Board of County Commissioners has the authority to act on any matter unless state law or the Ohio Constitution specifically prohibits the action. However, only taxes authorized by state law can be enacted and the county legislation cannot conflict with municipal or township legislation.

Both of the alternative forms require voter approval. A vote on establishment can be brought about in two ways: (1) the board of county commissioners may adopt a resolution to place an alternative form on the ballot; or (2) the board must submit an alternative form to the ballot if it receives a petition signed by three percent of the electors of the county. Either form can establish a number of members larger than three to serve on the county commission. Neither of the alternative forms disturbs the elected independent offices. Under an alternative form, no elected office can be abolished and no municipal powers can be gained.

Montgomery County tried in 1965 and again in 1971 to adopt

the appointed county executive form. Delaware County tried in 1991, Butler County in 1992, and Lorain County in 2000. The voters rejected the proposed plan every time.

The elected county executive plan has never been placed on the ballot.

County Administrators
The voters have denied both charter and alternative forms of county government. However, county commissioners in Montgomery and other urban counties needed help managing multi-million dollar budgets. In 1961, the General Assembly enacted a statute allowing a county commission to appoint, by a simple vote of the commission itself, an executive officer with the title, administrator. Today, about one-third of Ohio's counties have an appointed administrator. Appointment of an administrator does not confer any home rule powers on county government, nor does it affect the elected independent offices. The administrator is an employee of the county commission.

Developments Elsewhere
Article 10 of the Ohio Constitution states, in part, that ". . . the General Assembly shall provide by general law for the organization and government of counties." This means that the structure, offices, and responsibilities of county government as we know it today can be changed by the General Assembly or by the people through initiative legislation. No constitutional amendments are necessary to bring about such changes as: (1) reduction in the number of elected offices, (2) consolidation of management functions under a chief executive, and (3) establishment of a population-based formula to determine the number of seats on the county commission.

However, looking at the big picture, a constitutional amendment is necessary if basic changes are to be made in the total field of local government. Such an amendment is necessary to reduce the number of ways that a proposed county charter conferring municipal powers must be approved by the voters. The "hurdles" explained earlier in this chapter are a major obstacle to change not limited to traditional county functions and organization.

Examples of what might be good for Ohio exist in other states. *City-county consolidation* has occurred in such well known places as Boston, New Orleans, and Philadelphia. On the other hand, *city-county separation* can be found in Baltimore, Denver, St. Louis, and more than 30 cities in Virginia. In those places, what we think of as municipal services and county services are administered by one local government, not two.

Table 7-2: Number of Local Governments By State — How Ohio Compares With Those With Lowest Numbers (1997 Figures)

State	County	Mun.	Twp.	School	Special	Total
Ohio	88	941	1,310	666*	592	3,597
Virginia	95	231	0	1**	156	483
Louisiana	60	302	0	66	39	467
Maryland	23	156	0	0**	241	420
Delaware	3	57	0	19	257	336
Nevada	16	19	0	17	153	205
Alaska	12	149	0	0	14	175
Rhode Island	0	8	31	4**	76	119
Hawaii	3	1	0	0**	15	19

Notes: * Ohio includes City, Local, Exempted Village, Community College, and Joint Vocational School Districts.

   ** Virginia, Maryland, Alaska, Rhode Island, and Hawaii: all or most public school systems are attached to county or municipal governments.

Only the following six states have more local governments than Ohio: Illinois, Pennsylvania, Texas, California, Kansas, and Minnesota.
Source: 1997 Census of Governments, U.S. Bureau of the Census

The options for study are indeed numerous. Most states do not have township governments. New England counties are fading away. County governments exist in Vermont primarily to maintain a courthouse and jail. There are no county governments in Connecticut or Rhode Island.

There is no "correct" number of local governments within a state. Since the study of government is not an exact science, the "correct" number should be determined by a consensus of the citizenry. Ohio has more than 3,500 local governments. Yet, the states of Maryland and Virginia, each with roughly half the population of Ohio have approximately one-eighth as many local governments. Are the people of Ohio better off because they have so many more local governments?

These and other variations of local government are included in this text for study and consideration. The *County Home Rule Amendment* to Ohio's Constitution contains great potential for innovative change. Don't be fooled by the title: the County Home Rule Amendment is a key to the restructuring of all local government, not just county government.

Chapter 7 Review

■ Summary

The Ohio Constitution was amended in 1933 to allow (1) county home rule, and (2) alternative forms of county government. The County Home Rule Amendment allows the people to make significant changes not only to county government but also to township and municipal governments.

There have been numerous attempts to enact Ohio home rule charters. Authorization to form a charter commission can be placed on the ballot either by the county commission or by petition from county electors (voters). Ten Ohio counties have tried and failed to draft and/or adopt a charter: Columbiana, Cuyahoga, Franklin,

Hamilton, Lake, Lucas, Mahoning, Montgomery, Stark, and Trumbull. One Ohio county has succeeded: Summit.

Reasons for maintaining the current system of government (the *status quo*) include: voter apathy, lack of understanding of local governments, opposition to change by politicians, and the difficulty of obtaining voter approval of proposed county charters that confer municipal powers.

A *municipal power* is something that municipal governments can do and non-charter county governments cannot do. When municipal powers are involved, approval must be granted by a majority of voters: (1) in the county, (2) in the largest municipality, (3) in the county outside of the largest city, and (4) in each of a majority of the combined total of municipalities and townships in the county. The fourth requirement does not apply to counties with a population of 500,000 or more.

Two alternative forms of county government are available. They can be placed on the ballot either by the county commission or by citizens' petition. One alternative form is the elected county executive and the other is the appointed county executive. Both forms allow an increase in the number of county commissioners. The appointed county executive form has been voted upon but rejected in the counties of Butler, Delaware, Hamilton, Loran, and Montgomery.

Approximately one-third of Ohio's county commissions employ a person known as a county administrator. The administrator can bring professionalism to the job but he or she has no authority over elected independent offices. The appointment of an administrator does not bestow any home rule powers.

In other states, some counties are acting like cities and some cities are acting like counties. In those states, a layer of government has been eliminated. Efforts are being made to bring order and efficiency into the patchwork that is local government in the United States. Ohio has not joined that quest.

■ Glossary

City-County Consolidation. The merger of county government with other local governments within a county to form one unit of government.

City-County Separation. Political and functional separation of the city from the county. The city provides services traditionally provided by both the city and county governments.

Civil Service. A personnel system intended to hire and protect the employment of persons selected on the basis of merit instead of political loyalty.

Elector. A person who is registered to vote.

Lobbyist. A person who is paid by an employer to influence legislation and the decisions of public officials. Lobbyists are often referred to as the "third house" of the legislature.

Patronage. The power to award employment and contracts to supporters of the political party in office.

Political Boss. A political leader who controls a state or local party organization for personal gain, not to benefit the public. The party organization headed by a political boss is called a *political machine*.

Purchasing Agent. The official in charge of buying goods, services, and equipment for a government or private business.

Spoils System. The award of government jobs to political supporters and friends.

Urbanization. The transformation of living conditions from rural to urban (like a city).

■ Review Questions

1. The handing out of government jobs to political helpers is known as the _____ system.
2. A personnel system intended to recruit and keep qualified government employees is known as _____ _____.
3. Does the County Home Rule Amendment to the Ohio Constitution deal with county government only?
4. Does it take a constitutional amendment to eliminate one or all of the independent, elected county offices?
5. How many Ohio counties have a home rule charter?
6. In what two ways can adoption of a proposed county charter be brought to a vote of the people?
7. How many ways must voters express approval of a proposed county charter which confers municipal powers?
8. What are the alternative forms of county government which are made available by the state constitution?
9. Are there such things as consolidated cities and counties in other states?
10. Do all states have county governments?

Answers to Review Questions: 1. Spoils; 2. Civil service; 3. No; 4. No; 5. One; 6. By charter commission or by petition; 7. Four in counties with populations under 500,000, three in counties with populations of 500,000 or more; 8. Elected county executive and appointed county executive; 9. Yes; 10. No.

Chapter 8: THE MUNICIPAL LIFE CYCLE

Introduction

A municipality is born, it lives, and it dies. It is born when it is incorporated and it dies when it surrenders its corporate powers. A *corporation*, in the eyes of the law, is an artificial person. As an artificial person, a municipal corporation can function in the world of business.

It can, for example, enter into contracts, incur debt, sue in court, and be sued. Incorporated municipalities have their own government. The "unincorporated places" listed on some highway maps and in some U.S. Census Bureau publications are simply communities — usually very small communities — which have no government. In Ohio, these places are located in townships.

Incorporation

During the early years of Ohio statehood, the Ohio General Assembly passed a separate act (law) for the incorporation of each new municipality. Each act specified the form, organization, specific powers and functions of the new municipal government. The special act passed in 1838 for the incorporation of Jeffersonville is contained in Appendix A of this chapter.

Even though all Ohio municipalities were dealt with in the same manner (by separate act), they were not treated alike. Variations developed in the form of government and in the powers bestowed. What some municipalities were allowed to do, others were not. Because of the numerous differences and inequities, the General

Assembly found itself overwhelmed by municipal lobbyists seeking change.

Relief came when the Constitution of 1851 provided that "The General Assembly shall pass no special act conferring corporate powers." Municipalities were to be subject to *general* laws applicable to *all* municipalities. However, old habits die hard. State legislators decided to classify municipalities according to population and to enact laws applicable to specific population groups. For example, an act might apply only to municipalities with populations between 2,000 and 4,000. The practice became so prevalent and the groupings became so numerous that, in 1902, the Ohio Supreme Court ruled the classification system unconstitutional. It decided that legislating by multiple population groups was not much different than legislating by special acts.

The classification system in use today was established by a 1912 amendment to the Ohio Constitution. That amendment states, in part, that:

> Municipal corporations are hereby classified into cities and villages. All such corporations having a population of five thousand or over shall be cities; all others shall be villages.

Thus, in Ohio today we have municipalities called *cities* and municipalities called *villages*. The old familiar term, town, has no legal meaning.

The pre-1912 special incorporation acts specified the form, organization, specific powers, and functions of each new municipality (see Appendix A). Today, those specifications are found in Title Seven, "Municipal Corporations," of the Ohio Revised Code. The provisions in Title Seven apply to *all* villages and to *all* cities with one exception: those villages and cities which have created their own charters can manage their own internal affairs.

Incorporation of a Village

The land area of a proposed new village must be at least two square miles and must have a population of at least 800 persons per square mile. State law also requires that the area have an assessed valuation for property tax purposes of at least $3,500 per capita.

A petition signed by a majority of registered voters living in the area to be incorporated is presented to the board of county commissioners. The petition must include information such as a description and map of the land area involved and the proposed name of the new village. The county commission then holds a hearing during which people can speak for and against the proposed incorporation. Special attention is given to whether the new village will be able to provide services such as police and fire protection, streets, water, and sewers. If the commissioners find in favor of the petitioners, the incorporation becomes effective when notification is given to the Ohio Secretary of State. Officers of the new village government are elected at the next general or special election.

The incorporation procedure becomes more complicated when the proposed new village is within three miles of an existing municipality. Incorporation cannot take place unless (1) the nearby municipality has recently refused to *annex* the area in question (to expand its borders to include the area), or (2) the nearby municipality does not object to the incorporation.

Incorporation of a City

The land area of a proposed new city must be at least four square miles and each square mile must have a population of at least 1,000 people. The total population must be at least 25,000 and the assessed valuation of property for tax purposes must be at least $2,500 per capita.

Note that even though the Ohio Constitution defines a city as a municipality having 5,000 or more population, Ohio law requires a population of 25,000 or more for the incorporation of a *new* city. Thus, an area containing any number of people less than 25,000 is treated like a prospective village. Sponsors of incorporation must obtain approval from nearby municipalities, some of which may have a population of only several hundred people.

Application for incorporation of a city is, like that of a village, made by petition to the county commission. The petition must be signed by at least 20 percent of the *electors* (people who are registered to vote) of the territory. The three-mile restriction for villages noted above does not apply to the incorporation of a city. Nearby municipalities cannot object to the creation of a new city. If the county commission, after holding a public hearing, finds everything in order, the issue is placed on the ballot for determination by the voters who live in the area involved.

Figure 8-1: Ohio's Ten Most Populous Cities

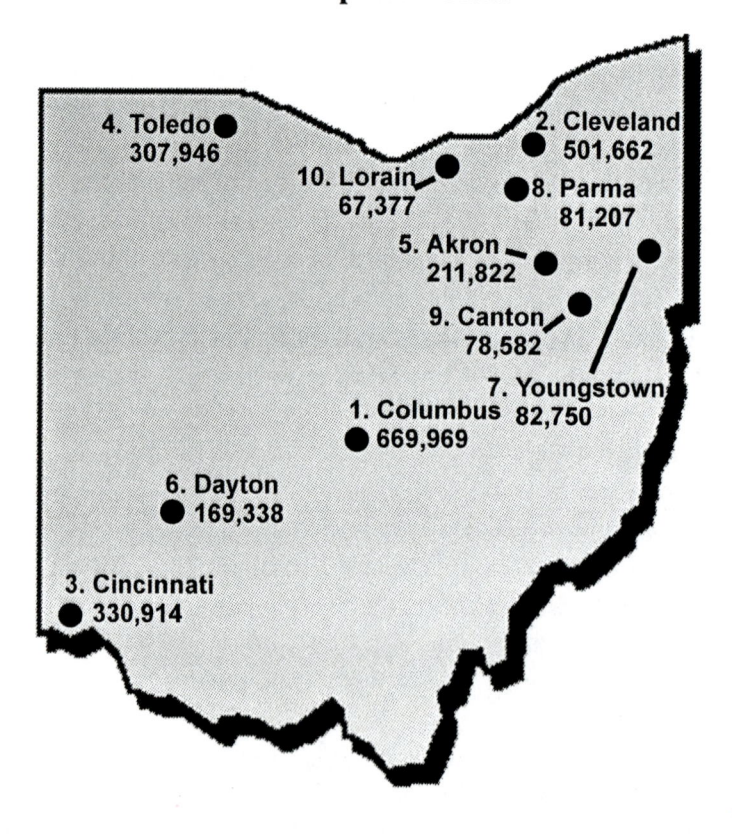

- 1. Columbus 669,969
- 2. Cleveland 501,662
- 3. Cincinnati 330,914
- 4. Toledo 307,946
- 5. Akron 211,822
- 6. Dayton 169,338
- 7. Youngstown 82,750
- 8. Parma 81,207
- 9. Canton 78,582
- 10. Lorain 67,377

An election is required for the incorporation of a city while no election is held for the incorporation of a village. Differences between city and village status are explained in the next chapter. Whether a city or a village, officers for the new municipality are selected by vote during the first general or special election held after incorporation.

The Municipal Life Cycle

Frequency of Incorporation

Sixteen Ohio municipalities were incorporated during the 1960s. Four were incorporated during the 1970s and five were incorporated during the 1980s. Four new municipalities were formed during the 1990s. The newest municipal corporations are outlined below in Table 8-1.

Table 8-1: Newest Municipal Corporations (As of May 2001)

Municipality	County	Year of Incorporation
Holiday City (village)	Williams	1997
New Franklin (village)	Summit	1997
Indian Springs (city)	Butler	1994
Highland Hills (village)	Cuyahoga	1990
Green (village)	Summit	1988
Huber Heights (city)	Montgomery	1981
Beavercreek (city)	Greene	1980
Buckeye Lake (village)	Licking	1980
Wayne Lakes (village)	Darke	1980

Incorporation of All or Most of a Township

Before 1967, it was relatively easy for the residents of a township to convert their township into a municipality. The residents simply formed a municipal corporation which encompassed all or most of the township area. However, in 1967, the state enacted anti-incorporation legislation establishing minimum requirements for incorporation. This legislation established the population per square mile requirement, the assessed valuation per capita requirement, and the three-mile restriction as described above. Backers of the anti-incorporation statute believed that township land would be annexed to existing municipalities as it became urbanized. Still, in the continuing tug-of-war between municipal and township interests, township trustees have clung to every square inch of township land whether urbanized or not. They have lobbied the General Assembly for and received ever increasing powers to govern in urban places. After more than a quarter of a century, it is unclear whether township or municipal interests have benefited more from the anti-incorporation policy. The policy is intended to benefit existing municipalities by encouraging annexation instead of incorporation of urban areas. However, municipal objections to incorporation within three miles of their borders can perpetuate the *status quo* and thus benefit the township.

Table 8-2 below contains a partial listing of municipalities which were formed before 1967 by incorporating all or most of a township. These municipalities stand out on a map by their square shape.

Table 8-2: Municipalities Formed From Whole Townships (Before 1967)

City	Square Miles	County
Avon	22.0	Lorain
Aurora	25.0	Portage
Brecksville	19.2	Cuyahoga
Mentor	28.0	Lake
North Ridgeville	25.0	Lorain
North Royalton	21.3	Cuyahoga
Oregon	28.5	Lucas
Parma	22.0	Cuyahoga
Strongsville	25.0	Cuyahoga
Solon	22.0	Cuyahoga

Since 1967, only Streetsboro in Portage County has been able to incorporate all or most of a township. Streetsboro contains 24.2

square miles and was formed in 1971. The latest attempt to incorporate most of a township took place in 1998 when residents of Jackson Township in Stark County made the effort. The new city was to be named Jackson Park but a large majority voted against incorporation.

Quasi-Corporations

County, township, and other local governments also must function in the world of business. They cannot incorporate. However, over a period of many years, specific powers have been given (one at a time) by the General Assembly to non-municipal governments. In fact, so many powers have been given that non-municipal local governments seem to operate quite well in the world of business. They, too, can buy goods and services, borrow money, and enter into contracts. Because they perform like a corporation, these other local governments are often called *quasi-corporations*. "Quasi" means "almost like" or "similar."

Annexation

The land area of a municipality can be increased by annexing or adding land. There are three ways by which municipal land area can be increased:

(1) A municipality can annex unincorporated (township) land (that is, land that is not inside another municipality).
(2) A municipality can transfer land to another municipality.
(3) Two municipalities or a municipality and a township can merge together.

Annexation of Unincorporated Land

The land to be annexed must be next to – and actually touch – the municipal boundary. The process can be started by either the owners of land located in the area under consideration or by the municipal council (legislature). If the municipal council starts the procedure, the issue is voted upon by the residents of the township. If the issue fails to be approved, the annexation of that particular land cannot be considered again for another five years. So, councils seldom start the procedure. Instead, they wait until landowners start it.

The Procedure Followed by Landowners

A majority of the landowners of the area under consideration submit a petition to the county commission. The petition requests annexation and contains relevant information, such as a legal description of the land involved. A public hearing is held by the commission to allow interested persons to speak for and against the request. The commission must find, among other things, that the annexation will benefit the area to be annexed. If the petition is granted, the area becomes a part of the municipality when it is formally accepted by the municipal council.

Annexations are often controversial. Petitions are frequently filed by land developers or other persons who seek municipal services for the land involved. Municipal officials usually welcome growth with the resulting increase in population, tax base, and land area. Township trustees frequently oppose annexations because they consider a municipal gain as a township loss. Even as this text is being updated (2001), the General Assembly is considering a bill which would make major changes to annexation procedures and requirements. See Appendix B, *The Annexation War of the Year 2000*, at the end of this chapter. Senate Bill 5 was introduced in January 2001 and is essentially the same as the bill considered in 2000.

Recent Annexations

An annexation can vary in size from one residential building lot to an area of many acres.

1,091 annexations took place during the four year period 1997-2000. During that period there were:

| No annexations in eight counties: | Erie, Hocking, Meigs, Morgan, Monroe, Portage Sciota, and Vinton. |

The Municipal Life Cycle

Less than 10 annexations in 48 counties:	Adams, Allen, Ashland, Ashtabula, Athens, Belmont, Butler, Carroll, Champaign, Columbiana, Coshocton, Crawford, Cuyahoga, Darke, Defiance, Gallia, Geauga, Guernsey, Hamilton, Hardin, Harrison, Henry, Highland, Holmes, Huron, Jackson, Jefferson, Lake, Lawrence, Logan, Madison, Mahoning, Marion, Mercer, Morrow, Muskingum, Noble, Ottawa, Paulding, Perry, Pickaway, Pike, Preble, Ross, Seneca, Van Wert, Washington, and Wyandot.
10 to 19 annexations in 21 counties:	Auglaize, Clark, Clermont, Clinton, Fayette, Fulton, Greene, Knox, Licking, Loraine, Lucas, Medina, Miami, Putnam, Richland, Summit, Trumbull, Tuscarawas, Union, Wayne, and Williams.

During the same period, there were also 11 counties in which 20 or more annexations took place. These annexations are outlined in Table 8-3 below:

Table 8-3: Counties Wherein 20 or More Annexations Occurred During 1997-2000

County	Number of Annexations	City or Village
Franklin	222	Columbus (147), Gahanna (20), Grove City (17), Hilliard (11), New Albany (7), Reynoldsburg (7), Dublin (7), Brice (2), Groveport (2), Westerville (2).
Wood	67	Perrysburg (30), Bowling Green (13), Rossford (11), North Baltimore (3), Pemberville (3), Walbridge (3), Fostoria (2), Tontogany (1), Grand Rapids (1)
Stark	43	Massillon (22), Louisville (6), Canton (5), Hartville (4), North Canton (3), Alliance (2), Navarre (1)

Table 8-3 continued on next page

Counties Wherein 20 or More Annexations Occurred During 1997-2000 (Continued)

Warren	41	Mason (11), Lebanon (11), Springboro (8), South Lebanon (5), Middletown (1), Orrville (1), Corwin (1), Franklin (1), Maineville (1), Carlisle (1)
Delaware	32	Columbus (10), Delaware (10), Westerville (5), Powell (4), Sunbury (1), Ostrander (1), Shawnee Hills (1)
Hancock	32	Findlay (31), Fostoria (1)
Fairfield	29	Lancaster (9), Pickerington (7), Canal Winchester (3), Thurston (2), Carroll (2), Columbus (1), Bremen (1), Pleasantville (1), Reynoldsburg (1), Lithololis (1), Baltimore (1)
Sandusky	25	Fremont (13), Belleview (9), Gibsonburg (2), Woodvillle (1)
Shelby	23	Sidney (10), Ft. Loramie (5), Botkins (3), Russia (2), Port Jefferson (2), Jackson Center (1)
Brown	20	Mt. Orab (10), Georgetown (7), Sardinia (2), Russellville (1)
Montgomery	20	Centerville (5), Dayton (5), New Lebanon (3), Miamisburg (3), Carlisle (2), Germantown (1), Moraine (1).

Transfer of Land Between Municipalities

A zig-zag or otherwise unusual boundary between two municipalities can cause problems. In emergency situations, for example, a home owner might call the wrong fire department or the firefighters might have trouble finding the home. Minor adjustments in boundary lines can be made voluntarily by the municipalities involved. Each must pass an ordinance agreeing to the change. The adjustments are finalized when the ordinances are filed with the board of county commissioners. Boundary line adjustments are noncontroversial; they don't happen unless everyone involved is in agreement.

Merger

Municipal to Municipal Merger

Municipal-township merger was described in Chapter 5. It is also possible for two municipalities to merge. The same two-step procedure is used. First a merger commission is elected to draft the proposed terms of the merger. Second, one year later, the proposed terms are accepted or rejected by the voters of both jurisdictions.

Below is a list of municipal to municipal mergers which have taken place over the last 55 years.

Table 8-4: Municipal to Municipal Mergers Since 1945

Municipalities Merged	County	Year
Basil, Baltimore	Fairfield	1945
South Bolevards, Mansfield	Richland	1948
Fairfield, Osborn*	Greene	1949
Roscoe, Coschocton	Coshocton	1957
Hanford, Columbus	Franklin	1958
Lakeville, Conneaut	Ashtabula	1962
Parkview, Fairview Park	Cuyahoga	1966
Shanesville, Sugarcreek	Tuscarawas	1967
Westview, Olmsted Falls	Cuyahoga	1971
Chippewa on the Lake, Briarwood Beach	Medina	1996

* Fairfield merged with Osborn and the name changed to Fairborn.

A strong argument can be made in support of the merger procedure, especially when the issue is between townships and municipalities. Unlike annexation, there are no adversaries. People can negotiate the terms and conditions under which merger will be acceptable to both jurisdictions. The voters can then decide whether the proposed merger is likely to bring about a better community.

Detachment

Municipalities can not only grow in land area, but they can also shrink. Land can be detached or removed. This practically never happens, but state law provides three methods by which it can.

First, the owners of the land involved can make the request (by petition) to the board of county commissions. If the city or village council agrees to the detachment, the board of county commissioners can grant the request. If detachment is granted, the land will either be added to an existing township or included in a new township.

Second, the land owners in a village can place the question of detachment on the ballot. The area involved must have at least 1,500 acres and it must be contiguous to an adjoining township. Only the owners of land in the disputed area can vote on the question. If detachment is approved, the land will either be added to an existing township or included in a new township. Land owners in a city do not have this option.

Third, if farm land is annexed but not developed in any way within five years, the owner can ask the court of common pleas to detach the land. The court has authority to grant the request.

Calling It Quits: Dissolving a Municipality

A municipal corporation can also be dissolved. The process is legally known as the *surrender of corporate powers*. Municipal residents can circulate a petition and place the issue on the ballot. The issue is: Shall the Village of _____ surrender its corporate powers? If a majority votes "yes," the municipal government is dissolved and the township government becomes responsible for providing necessary services. The following villages

The Municipal Life Cycle

have been dissolved: Halls Corner (Trumbull County), Lake Milton (Mahoning County), Sagamore Hills (Summit County), and Darbydale (Franklin County). These villages are only memories today. The latest vote on the subject took place in the year 2000, when something different happened. The people of Craig Beach (Mahoning County) voted to retain their corporate powers.

People may decide to dissolve their village government when the tax base will no longer finance an acceptable level of services or when candidates cannot be found to run for village offices. Municipal governments, like other endeavors, demand time and effort from people. They die when the residents turn away.

✓ Did you know?

You can stay abreast of current and pending state legislation from your home or office.

The Legislative Service Commission (a state agency) maintains an inventory complete with written analysis and final disposition of every bill considered by the Ohio General Assembly since the 1997-1998 session. If you know the bill number (for example, Senate Bill 5) and year considered, you can view the material on your computer monitor, download it, or ask that it be mailed to you. The LSC website also provides a search function which enables you to conduct text searches for legislation on topics of interest to you.

Legislative Service Commission
77 South High Street, 9th Floor
Columbus, Ohio 43266-0342
Phone: (614) 466-3615
Web site: www.lsc.state.oh.us

You may also be able to obtain information on state-level legislation affecting local governments in Ohio by contacting the applicable service organization identified in this text (e.g., the Ohio Township Association).

Additionally, the entire Ohio Revised Code is on the State of Ohio's website (www.state.oh.us). To access the code from the state homepage, simply click 'Government', then 'Ohio Legislative Branch, and 'Ohio Revised Code.' You can perform full text searches, and view or download one code section at a time. Title 3 deals with counties, Title 5 with townships, Title 7 with municipal corporations, and Title 33 with education.

Chapter 8 Review

■ Summary

A municipal corporation can be described as an artificial person who is born (incorporated), lives (grows by annexation and merger or shrinks by detachment), and dies (surrenders its corporate powers). Incorporation is brought about by people who wish to establish a municipal government.

State law determines how municipalities can be incorporated. For villages, the process requires that a petition be presented to the county commission. The commission grants or denies the request. Incorporation of a city also starts with a petition to the county commission. However, the question of incorporation is referred by the commission to a vote of the people who live in the area under consideration. State law has imposed minimum land area and assessed valuation requirements upon proposed incorporations. It also allows existing city and village councils to veto the incorporation of villages within three miles of their borders.

The Municipal Life Cycle 149

Other kinds of local governments are called quasi-corporations. Unlike municipalities, they are not artificial people in the eyes of the law. However, over the years, state laws have allowed them to do many of the things done by municipal governments.

The "unincorporated places" listed on some highway maps and in some U.S. Census Bureau publications are communities without their own governments. In Ohio, these places are located in townships.

Annexation is the procedure followed by landowners to bring their land inside a municipality. It is initiated by petition to the county commission. The land area of a municipality can also grow by merger with another municipality or with a township. Unlike annexation, which causes conflict between municipal officials and township officials, the merger procedure has no adversaries. Both parties strive together to design the best possible community. The resulting merger plan is then voted upon by the people of both jurisdictions.

State law also provides procedures by which land can be detached from a municipality. However, this rarely happens.

People can also decide that they do not want their municipal government any more. They can vote to "surrender corporate powers." If a majority of the electorate vote in favor, the municipal government dies. The people in several small Ohio villages have, over a period of many years, decided to dissolve their municipalities.

■ Glossary

Annex (Annexation). To combine, unite, or join together. Land can be annexed to a municipality and thus become a permanent part of the land area of that municipality. *Annexation* is the term used to refer to the procedure involved.

Corporation (Municipal Corporation). An artificial person created by law. As a corporation, the municipal government can function in the in the world of business.

Debt. An obligation to return money. Local governments borrow money by issuing notes and bonds. Notes are short term debt. Bonds are long term debt. Both are formal acknowledgments of indebtedness and both promise to make payments to the note or bond holder until the indebtedness is eliminated.

Detach (Detachment). To separate from the land area of a municipality. *Detachment* is the term used to refer to the procedure involved. The opposite of *Annex (Annexation)*.

Merge (Merger). The consolidation of two municipalities or a municipality with one or more townships. *Merger* is the term used to refer to the procedure involved.

■ Review Questions

1. Is it legally correct to identify an Ohio municipality as a "town?"
2. Why are municipal governments incorporated?
3. Are any other kinds of local government incorporated?
4. Who, in addition to a municipal council, can initiate annexation of land?
5. What is it called when two municipalities or a municipality and a township become a single government?
6. Can two abutting municipalities trade land?
7. Can the residents eliminate their municipal government?
8. Is it easier or harder since 1967 to incorporate all or most of an entire township?
9. Is the same procedure used to incorporate both a village and a city?
10. Can land owners have their land detached from a city?

Answers to Review Questions: 1. No; 2. To conduct business; 3. No; 4. Owners of land to be annexed; 5. Merger; 6. Yes; 7. Yes; 8. Harder; 9. No; 10. No.

APPENDIX A

An Act to Incorporate the Town of Jeffersonville in the County of Fayette 1838

Sec. 1 Be it enacted by the General Assembly of the State of Ohio, that so much of the township of Jefferson, in the County of Fayette, as is comprised within the limits of the town plat of the town of Jeffersonville, together with all such additions as may hereafter be recorded thereto, be, and the same is hereby created a town corporate, and shall hereafter be known by the name of the Town of Jeffersonville.

Sec. 2 That it shall be lawful for the white male inhabitants of said town, having the qualifications of electors of the General Assembly, to meet on the second Monday of April next, and on the second Monday of April annually thereafter, and elect by ballot, one Mayor, one Recorder, and five trustees, who shall be householders, and shall hold their offices for one year, and until their successors are elected and qualified, and they shall constitute the town council.

Sec. 3 That at the first election under this Act, they shall choose, vivavoce[1], two judges and a clerk, who shall each take an oath or affirmation, faithfully to discharge the duties assigned them, and at all elections thereafter the trustees or any two of them, shall be judges, and the recorder, clerk; and at all such elections, the polls shall be open between the hours of ten and eleven A.M. and close at three o'clock P.M. of said day, and at the close of the polls, the votes

---

[1] By voice vote

shall be counted and proclaimed, and the clerk shall deliver to each person elected, or leave at his usual place of abode, within three days thereafter, a written notice of his election, and the person so notified, shall, within ten days from the time of receiving such notification, take an oath or affirmation to support the constitution of the United States and of this state, and also an oath of office.

Sec. 4 The Mayor, Recorder, and Trustees, shall be a body corporate and politic, with perpetual succession by the name of the "Town of Jeffersonville", shall be capable of acquiring and holding real and personal property, and may sell and convey the same, may have a common seal, and may alter the same, may sue and be sued, plead and be impleaded, answer and be answered unto, in any court of law or equity in this state or elsewhere, and when any suit is commenced against the corporation, the first process shall be a summons, an attached copy of which shall be left with the Recorder, at least ten days before the term thereof.

Sec. 5 That the Mayor, Recorder, and a majority of the Trustees shall have the power to make such by-laws, ordinances and regulations for the health and convenience of said town as they may deem advisable, provided the same be not inconsistent with the constitution and laws of the United States, and of this state, and they shall have power to fill all vacancies occasioned by death, removal or otherwise, to appoint a treasurer, town marshal and such other subordinate officers as they may deem necessary, to prescribe their general duties, and to require such security as they may deem necessary to secure the faithful performance of those duties, to remove at pleasure, to fix and establish the fees of officers not inconsistent with this act.

The Municipal Life Cycle

Sec. 6 The Mayor shall be a conservator of the peace within the limits of said corporation and shall have the jurisdiction of a Justice of the Peace therein, in criminal and civil cases, and shall receive the same fees as Justices of the Peace are entitled to for similar services, he shall give bond and security, as is required of Justices of the Peace, and appeal may be taken from the decisions of the Mayor to the Court of Common Pleas, in the same manor as appeals are taken from the decision of Justices of the Peace.

Sec. 7 It shall be the duty of the recorder to keep a true record of the proceedings of the town council, which record shall at all times be open for the inspection of the electors of said town and the recorder shall preside at all meetings of the corporation in the absence of the Mayor, and shall perform such other duties as may be required of him by the by-laws and ordinances of said corporation.

Sec. 8 The Town Council shall have power to levy a tax annually for corporation purposes, on the property within the limits of said town returned on the grand levy, made subject to taxation by the laws of the state: provided that said tax shall not exceed in any one year three mills on the dollar, and the Recorder shall make out a duplicate thereof, charging each individual an amount of tax in proportion to his property as assessed on the grand levy of taxation, which said duplicate shall be certified and signed by the Mayor and Recorder and delivered to the Marshal, who shall proceed to collect the same in the same manner, and under the same regulation as county treasurers are required by law to collect county and state taxes; and said Marshal shall, as soon as said tax is collected pay the same over to the treasurer of the corporation.

Sec. 9 That said Town Council may appropriate any money in the treasury for the improvement of the streets and sidewalks, or other improvements, and may have the use of the jail of the county for the imprisonment of persons liable to imprisonment, and all persons so imprisoned, shall be under the care of the sheriff as in other cases.

Sec. 10 That the Mayor and Common Council shall have power to require by ordinance, each able bodied male person above the age of twenty one years, resident within said town to perform labor on the streets and alleys of the same, not exceeding two days in any one year, and which shall be in lieu of two days labor required under the present laws regulating roads and highways, and upon refusal or neglect to perform such work under the proper supervisor, the delinquent shall be liable to the same penalties as are provided by law against persons refusing to perform the two days labor required in said law; they shall also have the exclusive right of forming the road districts within the limits of said corporation and the appointment of suitable supervisors for such districts when formed, who shall be governed in the performance of their duties, by the by-laws of said corporation, and all road tax charged in the county duplicate on property within the limits of said town shall be worked out under the direction of the proper supervisors, within said town, as the said town authorities may, by resolution, designate and point out, and all taxes charged for road purposes as foresaid on property within the limits of said town, and collected by the county treasurer, shall be paid into the hands of the town treasurer aforesaid to be specially appropriated by the Mayor and Common Council to road purposes within said town.

C. Anthony
Speaker of the House of Representatives

George J. Smith
Speaker of the Senate

March 17th, 1838

The Municipal Life Cycle   **155**

I Jacob Creamer Recorder of the corporation of the Town of Jeffersonville, Fayette County, Ohio, do certify the forgoing to be a true copy of the charter of said town.

Given under my hand this 14th day of April. A.D. 1845

Signed: Jacob Creamer T. Recorder

I, R.B. Miller having been lawfully appointed by the Mayor and Council and duly sworn to transcribe and codify the ordinances of the village of Jeffersonville, Ohio, hereby certify the foregoing to be a true copy of the old record found on pages 1-2-3 & 4 of said record.

July 10th 1884
Signed: R.B. Miller

APPENDIX B

The Annexation War of the Year 2000

The word "feud" describes the municipal-township relationship when it comes to matters of annexation. Perhaps the best known feud was between the Hatfield family of Logan County, West Virginia, and the McCoy family which lived close by in Pike County, Kentucky. Their often deadly hostilities lasted for 31 years (1860 - 1891). In Ohio, pro-municipal and pro-township interests have been feuding with one another – in a more civilized way of course – for much longer than that. The bone of contention is annexation. Municipal interests love it. Township interests hate it. Why? They hate it because it usually results in the loss of land and tax revenue.

An uneasy truce was established in 1967 when municipal interests gained a new annexation law which tended to favor municipal governments. At the same time, township interests gained a new law controlling municipal incorporation which tended to favor township governments. Lobbyists on both sides lost something but also gained something. This is the old "you scratch my back and I'll scratch yours" credo of the lobbyists. Nobody gets hurt.

The trustees and supporters of over 1,300 townships are extremely effective lobbyists. Municipal people observe, jokingly but enviously, that township people have nothing to do while the fields are under snow, so they pass the time traveling to Columbus to badger the members of the General Assembly for pro-township legislation. They have succeeded rather well except in the realm of annexation. Proposed annexation laws, one after another, year after year, have failed to clear the General Assembly.

The Ohio General Assembly consists of a 99 member House of Representatives and a 33 member Senate. Tragedy (from the viewpoint of many special interest groups and their lobbyists – not to mention members of the General Assembly) struck in 1992 when

Ohio voters approved term limits for members of the General Assembly. Under the term limit amendment, Senate members are limited to two consecutive four-year terms and House members are limited to four consecutive two-year terms. The year 2000 became significant because term limits became operative that year. The limits required that 75 House members and eight Senate members leave the General Assembly at year's end. Looking into the future, 17 House members and 17 Senate members must leave at the end of 2002 while six House members and four Senate members must leave at the end of 2004. This great exodus takes with it the fruits of past lobbying efforts. Thus, the year 2000 was selected by township interests for an intensive, all-out push for what they called annexation reform.

The last several bills introduced to change the annexation law cleared the House only to die in the Senate. The new strategy was to clear the Senate first. Influential members of the Senate who favored change prevailed upon Ohio Municipal League and Ohio Township Association staff members to hold negotiations during 1999. The aim was to achieve an "agreed upon" bill, because when contending parties agree on the terms of a bill, the proposed legislation becomes non-controversial. The two organizations were asked to compromise on as many issues as possible. They were told that the Senate members would decide unresolved disputes.

Literature abounds concerning how lobbyists try to influence and even manipulate legislators. There are times however, when legislators find it to their advantage to influence and even manipulate the lobbyists. The desire is easily realized because an uncooperative lobbyist can lose his or her future effectiveness. When asked to jump through a hoop, most of them will. Enactment of "reform" legislation: (1) would allow many term limited legislators to leave office as heroes to their rural friends and associates, (2) would end the township-municipal annexation feud – at least for awhile, and consequently (3) would relieve future members of the General Assembly from endless hours of annexation badgering – at least for a few sessions. Whether specific proposed changes were good or bad, wise or unwise, was debated at length during Senate hearings but preexisting biases were not changed.

Annexation "Reform"

The year 2000 anti-annexation statute, labeled Senate Bill 289, was a complex measure containing four different annexation procedures. A companion bill, House Bill 98, was also introduced to educate the members of the House and thus to ensure swift action when S.B. 289 finally cleared the Senate. What follows is not an analysis of those bills but is instead a disclosure of concepts reflected in the proposed legislation.

1. Role of County Commissions

The current role of County Commissions when considering the adequacy of annexation petitions is ministerial (administrative) in nature. If the criteria listed in state statute is complied with, the annexation must be approved. The focus is on the question of whether the "general good of the area sought to be annexed will be served". "Reform" would give the commissioners a more judicial role. Their scope of consideration would be expanded to consider the effect of a proposed annexation on township land outside of the area to be annexed. They would also be required to conduct more formal hearings complete with, among other specifications, sworn testimony and subpoenas. Annexation cases could be decided (approved or disapproved) not only on the basis of benefit for some land owners but also on the basis of perceived harm to other land owners and to the township as a governmental entity.

2. Role of Township Trustees.

Township trustees have little to say about a pending annexation. They can, at times, argue that the area to be annexed is too large or that the township government can provide necessary services to the land being considered for annexation. However, this is seldom the case since very few townships can guarantee a dependable water supply or sewage disposal system.

Carrying the judicial analogy further, "reform" would cast the township trustees as the defenders of the *status quo*. Thus, it would be up to the owners of land to be annexed and municipal officials to prosecute or make the case for annexation. In effect, annexation hearings would focus on "the general good of the area to be annexed" versus "the general good of the township." S.B. 289 was silent about the effect of annexation on the municipality involved. That matter would not be considered by County Commissions when performing their judicial-like duties.

3. Township-Municipal Agreements.
The idea here is to require that township and municipal officials must agree to the terms of a pending annexation. Since the municipal officials would obviously favor the annexation, township officials would be in a position to control, for example, whether annexed land is withdrawn from the township and, if so, what reparations would be paid by the municipality to the township for lost tax base. S.B. 289 established a standard 15-year payback (reparations) schedule for use under certain circumstances when withdrawal did take place.

When S.B. 289 cleared the Senate on September 20, 2000, it was supported by The Ohio Township Association and the County Commissioners Association of Ohio together with their loyal following. Opponents included organized groups of realtors, builders, developers and other business interests. The Ohio Municipal League declared its opposition shortly after the bill was introduced. An ad hoc coalition of municipal governments (organized by a City Manager) strove mightily to mitigate features perceived to be especially objectionable. Nevertheless, the smart money was on swift approval by the House. After all, hadn't the House approved numerous anti-annexation bills only to see them die in the Senate?

As the days of the 123rd General Assembly dwindled down to a precious few, the bill received committee approval in the House on December 5, 2000. However, House Speaker Jo Ann Davidson found herself unwilling to support the bill. Without her backing, there was not enough support to bring the bill to the House floor for a vote. Senate Bill 289 died when the General Assembly adjourned on December 12, 2000. The word from township supporters was,

"Just wait until next year!"

Chapter 9: OHIO MUNICIPAL GOVERNMENT

Introduction

Almost every kind of local government has a single, well defined structure. All public school districts, for example, have the same basic form. Anywhere in Ohio, we can expect to find an elected school board which establishes policy and an appointed superintendent who carries out that policy. Sameness is also true of township governments, non-charter county governments, and even special purpose district governments. Local circumstances have nothing to do with the structure of those governments. It matters not whether they are located in urban or rural places or whether their territories are economically depressed or prosperous. A commercial for those local governments might advertise: "One size fits all." However, an exception to the sameness rule does exist. That exception is municipal government.

Figuratively speaking, citizens of Ohio can order off the menu or they can prepare their own municipal government. As used here, the "menu" is the Ohio Revised Code, which contains state laws of a permanent nature. Development of a charter gives citizens the opportunity to prepare a custom-made municipal government.

Before browsing through the menu or exploring the custom possibilities, however, we must consider the primary feature which distinguishes one form of municipal government from another. That feature is the *chief executive officer*, the person in charge of the executive branch of the government. More than anything else, it is the office of the chief executive which distinguishes one form of municipal government from another. Municipal chief executives in Ohio are either mayors or managers.

The Municipal Chief Executive Officer
Mayor

Weak Mayor. The office of mayor, like many county offices, goes far back into European history. It was brought to this country by the early settlers, and because they did not trust government, very little authority was given to the office. Note that in the incorporation statute shown in Appendix A of Chapter 8, the Mayor of Jeffersonville during the 1830s was a minor judge, but he did not have exclusive authority in other matters. He had no veto power or ability to appoint and remove other executive branch officials on his own. Instead, the statute tends to group the mayor, recorder, and trustees (council) together by stating that "they" shall have authority to do certain things. The Jeffersonville incorporation statute established what is known as the *weak mayor* form of government. The weak mayor form was used for large and small municipalities throughout the United States during the 19th century.

Those who favor the weak mayor form of government like the fact that executive power is diluted. They also like the fact that more than one official with executive power is elected. This, it is claimed, is not only democratic, but also wise. The elected executives can monitor one another. Opponents of the weak mayor form claim that cooperation among the elected executive officials can and does break down. When that happens, little can be accomplished. Opponents also argue that there is a lack of leadership and small likelihood that someone who knows how to manage a municipal government will be elected mayor.

Strong mayor. The close of the 19th century was a time of trouble and strife for many large cities. Those which could not provide adequately for the health, safety, and well-being of their burgeoning and diverse populations fell victim to machine politics and bossism. (See Chapter 7.) A *political machine* is a small group of leaders who control a major political party on the local level and use their positions for personal gain. They further their own interests, not the public good. Each machine is ruled by a *boss*. Although somewhat different in each community, bossism brought bribery, graft, and disorder to many big city governments throughout the country. Cleveland was for a time ruled by Boss Mark Hanna; Cincinnati was ruled by Boss George Cox.

Citizen opposition to bossism produced the *strong mayor* form of government. Reformers believed that strengthening the office could give the community a leader who would match or exceed the political boss in stature. The election of strong mayors who were on the side of good government would, they believed, provide opportunities to smash the political machines. In 1880, the City of Brooklyn, New York, adopted a strong mayor form and, in 1898, New York City followed. From there, it spread throughout the country.

Under the strong mayor system, the main features of the weak mayor form were reversed. The mayor was given veto power. The number of elected executive positions was reduced and the mayor was given the authority to hire and fire management staff. The strong mayor, a responsible leader politically accountable to all the people, could act as a foil to the political machine.

Those who favor the strong mayor form claim that it gives the chief executive both the responsibility and authority for running the municipality. Political leadership comes from inside, not outside, city hall. Opponents argue that elected chief executives must pay too much attention to political considerations and that people who run for the office might know very little about how to manage a municipal government.

Manager

The *council-manager* form of government is another product of the turn of the century reform movement. In 1908, the municipal council in Staunton, Virginia, appointed a "general manager" to run the city. If, they thought, private corporations like the Ford Motor Company or Sears Roebuck and Company are managed by professionals, why not municipal corporations? The Staunton experiment did not produce the council-manager plan as we know it today, but it did contribute to its development.

More detailed information on the council-manager plan is included later in this chapter when we introduce Richard S. Childs. Childs is known as the father of council-manager government. In summary, the plan features a small elected council which determines policy and a manager appointed by council to carry out its policies. Major differences between the council-manager form and the strong mayor form are: (1) the strong mayor is elected, while the manager is appointed, and (2) the strong mayor is independent from council, but the manager is dependent on council.

Those who favor the council-manager plan point out that responsibility is easy to pinpoint. If residents don't like *what* is being done, council is at fault. If they don't like *how* things are being done, the manager is at fault. The appointed manager can be recruited and selected on the basis of ability. Applicants for the position need not be residents of the municipality before appointment. Opponents of the plan argue that the people should be able to elect the chief executive officer. They wonder whether a manager hired from somewhere else can understand their community. Opponents also cite a lack of political leadership under the manager form.

Commission
Still another product of the turn of the century reform movement was the *commission* form of municipal government. It is mentioned here for historical purposes and because of its significance to the council-manager form. Under the commission form, a small number of commissioners (perhaps three or five) were elected. Each commissioner was in charge of a municipal function such as public safety, parks and recreation, public works, and so on. The commissioners served in both the executive and legislative branches of the municipal government. In their individual capacities, they were each an executive in charge of daily operations. As a group, they were legislators. The plan was tried and abandoned by several southern cities before 1900.

When a hurricane devastated Galveston, Texas in 1900, the commission plan of government was revived. It proved capable of producing quick results in an emergency. Later, in 1907, the commission plan was refined by Des Moines, Iowa by the addition of the initiative, referendum, recall, non-partisan elections, and civil service. This type of government became known as the Des Moines

Plan.

Ironically, the commission plan lost favor because it had, at the same time, both too much and too little centralization. It had too much centralization because both legislative and administrative powers were placed in the same hands. It had too little centralization because the executive branch is divided into parts (one part for each commissioner, rather like county government with its segments for each elected official). The commission plan lost favor during the 1920s. In Ohio today, it is used only by the small resort village of Valley Hi in Logan County.

Richard S. Childs and Council-Manager Government

Richard S. Childs is known as the father of the council-manager plan of municipal government. Born in 1882 and a 1904 graduate of Yale, he waged an intellectual war against machine politics and bossism. Before age 30, he had won a place of honor in the history of municipal government.

Childs was a member of a socially prominent New York City family which was actively involved in civic and political affairs. Richard Childs and his father, William Hamlin Childs, were dedicated to the destruction of the political machine known as *Tammany Hall*. Tammany was the name of a fraternal organization. The New York City political machine, a faction of the Democratic Party, operated out of the hall owned by the fraternal organization. (Thus, the name Tammany Hall.)

"There is," the younger Childs wrote in 1910, "such a thing as political science although the lawyers and politicians who design city governments rarely recognize it." The starting point in Richard Child's reform effort was a question. What kind of an environment encourages machine politics and bossism? He identified three conditions which are normally present.

First, elective offices are not visible. There are so many offices that the average voter cannot be familiar with all of them.

Second, communication between the candidate and his *constituency* (people eligible to vote for the candidate) is difficult. The "unwieldy constituency," as he called it, impedes grass roots support.

Third, governments are not well integrated or rationally structured. He cited county government as the extreme "ramshackle mechanism."

Making full use of his family's wealth and social standing, Childs at age 27 formed the National Short Ballot Organization, which, as the name implies, advocated reduction in the number of elected offices. Prominent people including future U.S. President Woodrow Wilson affiliated with the organization.

While the name "Short Ballot" implies fewer elected offices and consequently reorganized governments, Childs also confronted the problem of the unwieldy constituency. Voters, he lectured, should focus on candidates, not parties. He prescribed non-partisan elections. In addition, he counseled that consideration should be given to the use of a method of election known as proportional representation, usually referred to as "P.R."

Proportional representation breaks the monopoly held by the major political parties. It is defined as "a system of election by which competing interests secure representation in government in proportion to the number of votes cast." The system is based on a single, transferable vote. To vote, a person ranks the candidates listed on the ballot, marking his first choice, second choice, and so on. The number of votes (quota) required to win a seat is calculated by election officials. Candidates obtaining sufficient votes to meet that quota are declared elected. No votes are wasted. Surplus votes for winning candidates and the votes for candidates eliminated for low vote totals are distributed according to the second and subsequent choices declared by the voters on their ballot. Votes are transferred in this manner until sufficient candidates have been declared elected to fill all elective seats. Proportional representation is popular in Europe, but it has never taken root in the United States. It has been tried in Ashtabula, Cleveland, Cincinnati, Hamilton, and Toledo, all current or former council-manager cities.

The Childs Model
The ideal municipal government, according the model developed by Childs in 1910, is remarkably uncomplicated. A brief outline of his model is listed below:

Mayor
- Ceremonial head of the city.
- Presides over council meetings.
- Does not possess veto power.
- Might better be called chairman of the council.
- Appointed by council from its membership.

Council
- The legislative body.
- Small in number and elected at-large on a non-partisan basis.
- Large cities should consider using proportional representation.
- Hires and fires the manager.

Manager
- Selected and hired by council.
- Serves as chief executive officer.
- Responsible to council *as a group*.
- Hires and fires all or most of the other executive officers.

"I was," Childs remarked years later, "the minister who performed the marriage ceremony between the council-manager plan as first thought of in Staunton, Virginia, and the commission plan in Des Moines, Iowa." Childs was fascinated by the commission form, especially as it was modified for Des Moines. It was proof that municipal government could be something else besides mayor and council. He called his creation the *commission-manager* form of government. This explains why the charters of some cities, including Dayton and Springfield, identify their form of government as commission-manager instead of the more familiar council-manager.

Selling the Plan

Childs' quest for better government was more than an academic exercise. His next step was to lobby state legislatures for enabling legislation. This was necessary because municipal governments could not use the plan until authorized to do so by state legislation.

At first, the New York state legislature refused to adopt his plan, but other legislatures were more receptive. The big break came in 1912 when the South Carolina legislature acted to authorize use of the commission-manager plan. The plan was adopted that year by the City of Sumpter to take effect on January 1, 1913. After that, the plan was off, as Childs stated, "like a bunch of firecrackers." Ten additional cities located in several states adopted the plan during 1913 and the first large city, Dayton, Ohio, adopted it effective January 1, 1914.

The statement of the 1913 Dayton Charter Commission to the citizens is shown as Appendix A of this chapter. Indications are abundant that the 1913 charter commission followed the path established by Childs. "We have," they stated, "taken a step in advance of the commission-governed cities and provided a remedy for the generally acknowledged defects of such forms." The statement then lists innovations such as (1) the short ballot, (2) non-partisan elections, (3) a manager selected by and responsible to the city commission, and (4) a logical and systematic organization of government.

By 2001, the council-manager plan (as it is called today) was in use by slightly over 3,000 municipalities in the United States. It had also spread to other countries including Australia, Canada, Germany, Ireland, Isreal, New Zealand, Sweden, and the United Kingdom.

Richard S. Childs died on September 26, 1978 at the age of 96.

> ✓ **Did you know?**
> The Ohio City Management Association is an organization of City and Village Managers and other professional administrators who are engaged in the operation of local governments in Ohio. The association conducts meetings and conferences and publishes a newsletter. Secretariat services are supplied by:
>
> Management Development Programs
> The Ohio State University
> 2100 Neil Avenue, Room 301
> Columbus, Ohio 43210-1144
> Phone: (614) 292-7731
> Website: www.ocmaohio.org

Ohio Statutory and Optional Forms of Government

Article 18 of the Ohio Constitution states, in part, that:

> General laws shall be passed to provide for the . . . government of cities and villages; and additional laws may also be passed for the government of municipalities adopting the same; but no such additional law shall become operative in any municipality until it has been submitted to the electors thereof, and affirmed by a majority of those voting thereon, under regulations to be established by law.

In other words, the state legislature was told to establish government for cities and villages. The resulting city and village forms of government are known as *general statutory forms*. The state legislature was also given permission to make additional forms of government available. The additional forms are known as *optional forms*.

Article 18 of the Constitution also provides that "Any municipality may frame and adopt or amend a charter for its government." As indicated in Chapter 2, citizens can design a custom-made form of government for their municipality. This alternative is in addition to the general and optional statutory forms.

General Statutory
State law provides the strong mayor form of government for cities and the weak mayor form for villages. Today, about five percent of the cities and 95 percent of the villages use the general statutory forms.

Optional Statutory
Students of Ohio municipal government need not spend too much time studying the optional statutory forms. The General Assembly has provided three, but they are used by only one city and by only one village. The optional statutory forms are described below.

Commission Form. Each commissioner serves as both legislator and administrator. In Ohio, only the small resort village of Valley Hi in Logan County uses the commission form.

City Manager Form. The optional statutory city manager plan is used only by Washington Court House in Fayette County. The other 95 municipalities with managers have charters and they designed their own council-manager form of government. The charter design usually follows the Childs model and standards set by the International City/County Management Association which is headquartered in Washington, D.C.

Federal Plan. The federal plan is not used by any municipality in Ohio. It is a form of strong mayor government, but it differs somewhat from the general statutory strong mayor plan. The major differences are:

- There are fewer elected offices (only the mayor and members of council are elected).
- Department heads, although subject to civil service rules and regulations, are given rather autocratic authority over organization and personnel within their respective departments.

- The chief legal advisor serves as acting mayor when the elected mayor is ill or away.

Under the general statutory plan for cities, the auditor, treasurer, and law director are also elected. Department heads have less control over personnel and organization and the president of council serves as acting mayor when the elected mayor is ill or away.

Charter Government

The general and optional forms of government can only be changed by the General Assembly. Any change affects every municipality operating under the form changed. For example, any change to the general statutory weak mayor form affects at least 650 villages. Any change to the general statutory strong mayor form affects a dozen cities. Proposed changes can encounter fierce opposition. What's good for one municipality isn't necessarily good for others. Should, for example, the chief fiscal officer be elected or appointed? Changes are hard to come by. Critics say that the statutory forms are inflexible and some even charge that they are "set in concrete." Consequently, there are now in Ohio 125 mayor-council charters, 96 council-manager charters, and 11 which require the mayor to appoint an administrator or director of administration.

Administrator or Director of Administration

In Ohio, there are 11 mayor-council charters which require the mayor to appoint a well-qualified person to direct the daily operations. The duties and authority of that position are usually defined in the charter which also assigns a title. This variation on the mayor-council form is viewed by its supporters as a compromise. It has, they claim, the best features of both the mayor-council and council-manager forms. The mayor can provide political leadership while the daily operations can be handled by a professional. Critics contend that each newly-elected mayor will want to choose his or her own person for the job. "Real professionals," they believe, are not interested in employment which depends on election results.

While 11 municipalities provide for administrators or directors of administration by charter, others have established the position by ordinance. About 70 villages and perhaps six cities have done so. A major difference between positions established by charter and those established by ordinance is that a position established by ordinance can be changed or eliminated more easily. What is established by ordinance can be changed or eliminated by ordinance.

Other Executive Offices

Executive officers carry out or "execute" policy. The chief executive officer of an Ohio municipality is either a mayor or manager. The chief executive, however, needs help which is provided by other executive officials, most of whom are responsible to the chief executive. Following is a brief introduction to officials who are usually to be found in municipal government.

Who's Who in City Hall

Auditor or Director of Finance. The elected auditor is the chief fiscal officer. This official accounts for revenues and expenditures, authorizes payments, inventories city-owned properties, and keeps a record of all city-levied taxes and assessments. Where there is no elected auditor, the city will have a director of finance appointed by the chief executive.

City Clerk/Clerk of Council. The clerk prepares minutes of council meetings, and is the custodian of council records including the city code of ordinances. The clerk also receives petitions and other communications intended for council consideration.

Treasurer. If there is no director of finance, an elected treasurer serves as banker for the city. The treasurer receives, has custody of, and disburses (pays out) the city's money.

Community Development Director. This official enforces regulations concerning how land in the city should be developed and used. The title *planning director* is used in some cities. Whatever the position is called, planning, zoning, and development are brought together in this office.

Director of Law. The director of law is elected in non-charter cities. A charter can make the position elected or subject to appointment by either the council or the chief executive officer. The director of law serves as lawyer for all municipal officials. Some law directors have the title *city attorney*; and still others have the title *solicitor*.

Director of Public Safety. The appointed director of public safety oversees the work of the police and fire chiefs. Thus, he or she is responsible for public safety, including emergency medical services.

Director of Public Service. This appointed official is responsible for just about everything the city builds or maintains. This includes streets, storm sewers, sidewalks, parks, playgrounds, and can even include utilities, such as water, waste water, and electricity. Trash collection and disposal can be another responsibility of the public service director.

Safety-Service Director. The safety director and service director positions are combined in some cities. The person holding the combined position is often regarded as second in command to the chief executive officer.

Personnel Director or Civil Service Commission. State law provides a personnel system called Civil Service which must be followed by statutory (non-charter) cities. Civil Service is another product of the turn of the century government reform movement. It prevents incoming office holders from replacing employees with people who helped them win election. Unless a position is specifically exempted, Civil Service requires recruitment based on merit and it provides job protection. The program is administered by a three-member Civil Service Commission which is appointed by the city's chief executive officer. Some cities with charters follow the state civil service laws while others do not. Those which do not follow the civil service laws will design their own personnel system, which is headed by an appointed official usually called the *personnel director*.

Who's Who in Village Hall

Board of Trustees of Public Affairs. If the village does not have a village administrator, the utilities (water, sanitary sewer, and electricity) are managed by an elected three-member board of trustees. The board employs a clerk who keeps its records and performs assigned tasks.

Village Administrator. Village council can eliminate the board of trustees of public affairs and replace it with a position entitled *village administrator.* This is done when the utilities require increased attention. More attention is necessary as the utilities expand to serve additional customers. There are, for example, personnel policies to develop, supplies and materials to purchase, contracts to let and administer, billings to be made, and ongoing supervisory responsibilities. The administrator is appointed by and is responsible to the mayor. He or she can be assigned other tasks, such as being purchasing agent for all village activities, in addition to the operation of utilities.

Clerk. The elected village clerk is the chief fiscal officer. The duties are similar to those performed by an elected city auditor. The village clerk also keeps the minutes of the council meetings and has custody of village records.

Fire Chief or Fire Prevention Officer. Villages can have both paid and volunteer fire employees. They can also provide emergency medical services. If a non-charter village does not have a fire department, state law requires that it appoint a fire prevention officer.

Marshal. This is what the village chief of police is often called. The marshal is appointed by the mayor unless a charter provides otherwise.

Street Commissioner. The appointed street commissioner supervises the improvement, repair, and maintenance of streets, sidewalks, alleys, and other village-owned facilities.

Treasurer. The elected village treasurer performs duties comparable to those of the city treasurer. They both receive, have custody of, and pay money. Village councils can combine the clerk and treasurer positions. In Ohio, there are many clerk-treasurers.

The Legislative Branch

Non-Charter Village Council

When a village has no charter, state law requires a six-member council. State law also requires that all six members be elected at-large for terms of four years. *At-large* means that the members can live anywhere in the village.

The four-year terms overlap one another. Overlapping terms are often called, "staggered" terms. Two members are elected during one municipal election and four are elected the next. This is intended to provide continuity (that is, to prevent sweeping changes in membership with resulting loss of experience).

The mayor serves as presiding officer during meetings of the council. The mayor has no veto power and cannot vote except to break a tie.

Non-Charter City Council

As indicated above, there is only one way to choose members of a non-charter village council. City residents, on the other hand, have a choice between two methods.

Alternative 1: The Method Established by State Statute

Council members serve two-year terms unless four-year terms have been authorized by the voters. When a city has a population of less than 25,000, state law requires a seven-member council elected on a partisan basis. Three members are elected at-large and four are elected by *wards*.

For election purposes, the land area of the city is divided into parts called wards. Each ward must contain about the same number of people. For example, four wards would contain about 5,000 people each in a city having a total population of 20,000. A candidate who wishes to represent a ward must be a resident of that ward. Voters can vote for all at-large candidates. However, only people who live in a ward can vote for a candidate running to represent that ward.

Those who favor election by wards claim that it ensures that all areas of the city are represented on council. Critics claim that the best qualified people should be able to run for council regardless of where in the city they live.

Cities with populations of 25,000 or more have councils with more than seven members. State law tells how additional members are chosen and elected. A sliding scale based on population provides for additional members of council as the population increases. The total number cannot exceed 17.

The official who presides over meetings of council has the title *president of council*, an office separate from that of *member of council*. Candidates run for the president of council office. The president of council has no vote except to break a tie. Terms are for two years unless four-year terms have been authorized by the voters.

Alternative 2: The Other Method

Either city council or the citizens, by initiative petition, can place another method of determining the composition of the council on the ballot. The alternative method can, among other things: (1) set the number of council members anywhere from five to 17, (2) provide four-year terms which can overlap, and (3) include or not include wards. The term of the president of council can also be set at four years.

Charter Councils

A municipal charter can deal with all of the above considerations. Whatever is thought best for the community can be written into the charter.

Mayor's Court

Hometown justice is still available in Ohio. It is dispensed by *mayor's courts* which are located in 432 cities and villages. As shown in the following table, most mayor's courts can be found in villages.

Table 9-1: Mayor's Courts

Population	Number of Mayor's Courts
Under 1,000	160
1,000 to 2,499	122
2,500 to 4,999	74
5,000 to 9,999	43
10,000 to 19,000	22
20,000 or more	11
Total:	432

The most serious cases such as murder or grand theft are not taken to mayor's court. The local mayor can only deal with violations of municipal ordinances or traffic laws. The alleged violation must have taken place inside the municipality.

People charged with a violation which can be heard by mayor's court have a choice. They can have their case heard in mayor's court or they can have the case transferred to a higher court. Mayors of non-charter municipalities have an even more basic choice: They can choose to operate a court or not operate a court. In other words, state law allows mayors to operate a court, it does not require them to do so. Mayors of charter municipalities will operate a court, so long as the state allows it and if the charter requires it.

Critics of mayor's court point to a potential conflict of interest because the mayor's decisions bring money into the municipal treasury. To avoid an appearance of conflict, an increasing number of municipalities appoint magistrates to preside over mayor's court. The magistrate, who has no other role in the municipal government, is usually an attorney. His or her compensation is not based on court decisions.

Other critics believe that only lawyers can dispense justice because they understand our complex legal system. Advocates claim that it does not take someone with a law degree to determine, for example, whether Mr. Jones has junk cars in his front yard.

With a mayor's court, Mr. Jones can have his case decided rather quickly without taking time off from work. Mayor's courts are usually held during the evening. Without a mayor's court, Mr. Jones probably has to drive to another city and the penalty can be not only a fine, but also the loss of a day's pay and the cost of travel and parking. Also, without a mayor's court, the zoning inspector or police officer who issued the citation must also travel to the other city to offer testimony.

Mayor's courts are a convenience for both the residents and the municipal government.

✓ Did you know?

The **Ohio Municipal League** is an association of cities and villages. It represents municipal interests before state legislative, administrative, and judicial bodies. The League conducts meetings and conferences, publishes newsletters and a magazine, and provides a reference service. Information concerning municipal government in Ohio can be obtained by contacting:

> The Ohio Municipal League
> 175 South Third Street, Suite 510
> Columbus, Ohio 43215-7100
> Phone: (614) 221-4349   www.omunileague.org

The League cooperates with and provides support services for the following organizations of municipal officials, which can be contacted through the League:

> Ohio Association of Public Safety Directors
> Ohio Municipal Attorneys Association
> Ohio Municipal Clerks Association
> Mayors Association of Ohio
> Municipal Finance Officers Association of Ohio

Chapter 9 Review

■ Summary

The Executive Branch. More than anything else, it is the executive branch which distinguishes one form of municipal government from another. Municipal chief executives in Ohio are mayors or managers.

All mayors are elected but, once in office, all mayors do not have the same authority. The so-called "strong" mayors can veto municipal legislation and they can hire and fire other executive officials who are subordinate to them. The "weak" mayors have no veto power and they must obtain the approval of council before appointing subordinate executive officials.

State statute requires that villages have the weak mayor form of government unless the residents enact one of the optional forms or approve a charter. Cities are required to have the strong mayor form unless the residents enact one of the optional forms or approve a charter.

Mayors of both cities and villages can conduct a mayor's court if they wish to do so. Mayor's court can hear cases involving violations of municipal ordinances and traffic offenses.

A manager, who is appointed by council, has no role in the legislative process. Council decides what to do, and the manager and his or her staff are expected to execute (carry out) that policy. Richard S. Childs (1882-1978) is known as the father of the council-manager form of government. He blended what he considered to be the best features of the commission form with a "general manager" experiment which was carried out at the turn of the century by Staunton, Virginia. This was not just an academic exercise: Childs took his plan to state legislatures and lobbied for state enabling legislation. That he was successful is reflected in the fact that over 3,000 communities in the United States now operate under the council-manager plan.

The Legislative Branch. Non-charter village councils have six members who are elected at-large. Terms are for four years and they overlap. The mayor serves as presiding officer during meetings of the council but has no vote except to break a tie. Residents of non-charter cities have a choice:

Alternative 1: The Composition Provided by State Statute. There are seven members of council in cities which have a population of less than 25,000. Three members are elected at-large and four are elected by wards. The president of council presides during meetings. The president has no vote except to break a tie. Terms are for two years.

Cities with populations of 25,000 or more have councils with more than seven members. A sliding scale based on population provides for additional members as the population increases. The total number cannot exceed 17.

Alternative 2: The Other Method. Either the council or the citizens can place another method of determining the composition of council on the ballot. The alternative method can, among other things, (1) establish the number of council members, (2) provide four year terms which can overlap, and (3) include or not include wards. The term of the president of council can also be set at four years.

Optional Forms of Municipal Government. Students of Ohio municipal government need not spend too much time studying the three statutory optional forms of municipal government. They are used by only one small village and by one city. The optional forms are entitled: (1) commission, (2) city manager, and (3) federal. They are not used to any great extent because the charter route to governmental change is available.

Charter Government. The general statutory and optional forms of municipal government can be changed only by the General Assembly. Any change affects every municipality operating under the form changed. Charters, on the other hand, allow individuality and relative ease of amendment. By 2001, Ohio had 125 mayor-council charters, 96 council-manager charters, and 11 which require the mayor to appoint an administrator or director of administration.

■ Glossary

Commission Form of Government. Both legislative and executive powers are exercised by a commission. The number of commissioners is usually small, perhaps three to five. Collectively, the commissioners constitute a legislative body. Individually, each is the administrator of one or more municipal executive departments.

Council-Manager Form of Government. A form of municipal government in which an elected council appoints a professional manager to administer the operational affairs of the municipality. Features of the plan include: (1) a small council of five to seven members, (2) a mayor with no executive duties, and (3) a manager with ability to hire and fire subordinates. Although charters can provide otherwise, elections are usually non-partisan.

Mayor-Council Form of Government. A form of municipal government in which a mayor is elected to serve as chief administrative officer and a council is elected to establish policy. Although charters can provide otherwise, elections are usually partisan.

Short Ballot. A ballot listing relatively few offices and candidates for election to those offices. This is a reflection of a belief that people have better control of government when only a few offices are filled by election. Voters can know more about each candidate.

■ Review Questions

1. Municipal chief executives have the title _____ or _____ .
2. Do Ohio village governments usually have the weak mayor form of government or the strong mayor form?
3. (True or false) Partisan elections are usually held under the mayor-council form of government.
4. Are Village and city managers appointed or elected to their offices?

5. Who is known as the father of the council-manager form of government?
6. What was the first large city in the entire country to adopt the commission-manager (council-manager) form of government?
7. (True or false) Non-partisan elections are usually held under the council-manager form of government.
8. Under what form of municipal government is each elected member of the legislative body also the head of an operating department?
9. If members of council are not elected by wards, they are said to be elected _____.
10. Are mayors required by state law to operate mayor's courts?

Answers to Review Questions: 1. Mayor or manager; 2. Weak Mayor form; 3. True; 4. Appointed; 5. Richard S. Childs; 6. Dayton, Ohio; 7. True; 8. Commission form; 9. At-large; 10. No.

APPENDIX A

Statement of Charter Commission
1913

To the Voters of Dayton, Ohio:

We submit herewith for your consideration a proposed charter, framed under authority and in conformity with the constitution and laws of the State of Ohio.

In the preparation of the charter the Commission has sought information and suggestions from many sources. A number of public meetings have been held at which general discussion was had of what provisions the charter should contain. Charters of other cities have been carefully examined and considered. The Commission has incorporated in this charter all of the provisions which it believed would furnish the best charter for our city.

We have taken a step in advance of the Commission governed cities and provided a remedy for the generally acknowledged defect of such form. We have provided a chief administrative officer named "The City Manager," whose duty it shall be to supervise and control the conduct and operation of all officers and employees of the city and to manage the affairs of the city in an efficient and economical manner. We are convinced that this centralization of administrative authority will produce business-like methods in city government and fix responsibility for official actions that will result in great benefit.

To enable the voters to obtain a comprehensive view of the prominent provisions of this charter, we submit the following brief outline:

The Commission

The legislative functions are delegated to a Commission of five citizens, elected at-large by the people and any and all of whom are subject to recall at all times. At the first election three

Commissioners will be elected for four years and two for two years, and thereafter their successors shall be elected for four years. In this manner we insure a Commission at all times familiar with the operations of the city government.

The City Manager

A competent, experienced, trained and capable person selected on account of his peculiar fitness and ability to manage the affairs of the city.

Nominations and Elections

(1) Party politics are eliminated. No party designations will appear on the ballot.

(2) Ward lines are abolished. The city is considered as a unit, insuring to all parts of the city equal representation and consideration.

(3) The short ballot principle has been adopted.

(4) Elective officers and the City Manager are subject to recall by the people at all times.

Initiative and Referendum

Provision has been made whereby the people may initiate legislation and compel the submission to them of any legislation passed or refused to be passed by the Commission. This insures the control of all legislation to the people.

Civil Service Board

A civil service board of three will be appointed by the Commission for terms of six years, one appointed every two years. The Commission will have authority to see that all officers and employees are appointed on the basis of merit and fitness alone, and will keep a record of their efficiency in the service.

Administrative Departments

The various functions of the government are subdivided into departments all under the jurisdiction and control of the City Manager. The subdivision is logical and systematic and allows the greatest latitude for the efficient discharge of the functions of government. Each department will be in charge of a director selected by the City Manager on account of his fitness, integrity and ability.

Accounting and Finance

In creating the Department of Finance, great care has been exercised to provide for the institution of the best and most modern business methods of accounting. All of the financial affairs of the city are consolidated in this one department. Principles of accounting are laid down and the duty imposed in the Director of Finance to establish them for all administrative departments. An adequate system of accounting, such as herein provided, will prevent the waste of public funds and insure an adequate record of all municipal transactions. An independent continuous audit by certified public accountants, under the direction of the Commission is also provided, as well as complete compulsory publicity of all financial affairs.

Public Welfare

A department has been created for the purpose of developing and caring for the welfare of the people. We believe that the welfare of the people is as important as the care of their property. Public health, parks and playgrounds, charities and contributions, and recreation are gathered together in this department.

Legal Advertising

The charter provides a radical departure from the present custom in this regard. It is optional with the Commission to publish all legal notices in a paper published by the city or in a daily newspaper of general circulation. If the latter method is adopted, it shall be done by contract let only after competitive bid.

Franchises

No exclusive grants are permitted. The Commission may, by ordinance, grant franchises, but all ordinances making grants or renewals shall reserve to the city the power to regulate, the right to terminate, and to purchase the property of the utility.

City Purchasing Agent

All purchases made by the city are made by an agent appointed for that purpose, who shall purchase supplies after competitive bidding. This will provide an economical and efficient system for purchase of supplies.

In addition to the foregoing provisions, the charter provides:
1. A simplified election system.
2. Elective officials are directly responsible to the people.
3. Responsibility is definitely fixed.
4. An adequate system of accounting is established.
5. The rights of the city in matters relating to franchises and utilities are carefully guarded.
6. The merit system in appointments to public office is assured.
7. Full publicity of public records is provided.
8. Public depositories and interest on public funds is assured.
9. The manner of assessments for improvements has been clearly set fourth.
10. The Commission is given authority to settle damage claims without unnecessary cost.
11. An eight hour law for public work may be provided.
12. Improvements may be made by contract or by direct labor.

These and other features will provide a workable, simplified, and well-balanced system of government.

The members of the (Charter) Commission have adopted this charter by unanimous vote, believing that if it is adopted by the people, it will provide for Dayton an adequate, economical, and efficient form of government, and one that will be responsive to every demand of the people. The adoption of this charter by the voters will insure to the city a form of government devised to suit its particular needs. If adopted, we will not be compelled to continue under a form of government provided by the General Assembly, suitable to no particular city in the state, and which is antiquated, cumbersome, and wholly unsuited to the needs of a modern, progressive city like Dayton.

The people of Dayton must chose between the present form of government and the form expressed in this charter.

THE CHARTER COMMISSION
(Signed by 15 members of the charter commission)

Chapter 10: PUBLIC SCHOOLS

The Early Years

"Religion, morality, and knowledge, being necessary to good government and happiness of mankind, schools and the means of education shall be forever encouraged." These are the words of the Northwest Ordinance of 1787. To provide money and support for education, the Continental Congress had reserved one thirty-sixth of all the land in the Northwest Territory for school purposes. This grant of land was written into the Land Ordinance of 1785. In a surveyed township containing 36 sections (36 square miles) this amounted to one section in every surveyed township. Every Section 16 was reserved for education.

It would be some years, however, before the school land program could begin to produce results. The creation of a public school system had to wait until state and local governments were in place. Until then, public education in the Northwest Territory depended on subscription schools.

Subscription Schools
Public schools used to be called *common schools*. In 1789, a free common school was established in Marietta. It was established by a private company which was formed to settle military veterans on land in and around what is now Marietta and Washington County. The first teacher was a minister: The Reverend Daniel Story. He preached on Sunday and taught school during the week. Settlers who did not live close to Marietta were not so fortunate. They had to turn to *subscription schools* if they wanted to obtain an education for their children.

Teachers, during territorial days, were independent business people. Early school masters, as the title implies, were men. Settlers subscribed for their teaching services by agreeing to pay a sum of money. Teachers who settled in a community usually obtained room and board from a local family. Teaching on the frontier was not the life for a lady. If too few people in a community wanted the service, the school master moved on.

The First Hundred Years, 1803–1903

Fate of the School Lands Program

The Continental Congress set aside one thirty-sixth of the land in the Northwest Territory to benefit schools. The program had great potential. A 36th of all the land in Ohio amounted to over 1,100 square miles. That is equal in area to two counties! The sale of forest, mineral, and farm products from such a vast area could have been a great asset in building a public school system. However, the funds that could have been available from the land grants were, for all practical purposes, mishandled and lost.

While the school lands were given to the State of Ohio, program operation was placed in the hands of township trustees. Trustees in each township were made responsible for the 640 acres in their township. Thus, the custody of school lands was placed in the hands of people who had little or no formal education. Many trustees were ill-prepared for such a responsibility and, consequently, they made many mistakes.

State laws were enacted to regulate management of the school lands. Under these laws, the land would be leased and revenue received would be used for school purposes. Mismanagement, however, was rampant from the start. Not only did "city slickers" from the East get fantastically good deals but so did the friends and families of some township trustees. School lands, for example, were leased for long periods of time at extremely low rates. It was not unusual for a lease to run for 99 years and be renewable forever. Some business people, after signing a lease, simply cut the timber and abandoned the land. Other school lands were occupied by squatters who paid nothing.

After 23 years of bungling, the state legislature asked the U.S. Congress for permission to sell the school lands. Permission was granted as long as (1) people were allowed to vote on whether "their" land would be sold, and (2) the revenue from sales was placed in a state-administered common school fund. Interest earned by money in the fund would be paid to the township school districts which gave up the land. By 1828, the common school fund contained over $4,110,000. At that time, the state government owed a great deal of money for canal construction. The school money was borrowed and the state legislature promised to pay back annually *and forever* an amount equal to six percent interest. This became known as the irreducible debt. The irreducible debt, it turned out, was reducible. It was reduced to nothing in 1968 when Ohio voters approved liquidation of the trust fund.

The people in some townships declined to sell their school land and to participate in the common school fund. The custody of those lands remained in the hands of township trustees until 1917 when the auditor of state was made supervisor of school and ministerial lands in addition to his other duties.

"Section 16" school lands have practically disappeared. By 2000, there were slightly over 1,200 acres (1.87 square miles). Only Marion Township in Hardin County has retained all 640 acres. Today that land is being farmed. Smaller parcels of land are still held by Green Township in Ross County, Big Island Township in Marion County, and Madison Township in Franklin County. In addition, several small lots in Columbiana County are under leases for 99 years renewable forever.

Building a Public School System
The building of a public school system illustrates why state government needs local governments. The state legislature decides what to do and how that goal might be reached. It then assigns tasks to the local governments or it simply gives them the authority to do certain things. Some of the early actions taken to provide common schools are summarized in this section.

Civil townships were used as the first building blocks. In 1821, township residents were authorized to form township school districts. Property within each township was made subject to a property tax to support the local schools. However, the early school boards were not required to levy the tax and some did not. Children in townships with no school tax had no school to attend or they attended a subscription school. Some township districts levied such small amounts that the school closed, or had to revert to subscription, for a part of each school year.

In 1825, state legislators who were interested in schools struck a bargain with those who were interested in canals. A major canal law was passed one day and a major school law was passed the next. Each voted for the other's law. The 1825 law *required* township school boards to levy a tax for the operation of their schools. The fact that the tax was required made the law controversial. At the time, many people questioned the need for public schools. They doubted that their children needed reading, writing and arithmetic, and they objected to paying for the schooling of other people's children. The 1825 law also brought county government into the school system for the first time. Each county was required to establish a board of examiners to be sure that the teachers were qualified to teach.

State government was first given a role in 1837 when the position of State Superintendent of Common Schools was created and given to Samuel Lewis. In 1838, Lewis championed a state tax to help the common schools. At the same time, school boards were given the ability to borrow money. Many one-room schools were built with borrowed money.

Until 1847, all school laws applied uniformly to both rural and urban areas. No distinction was made until the *Akron Law* was enacted. Akron became the first city school district. The law allowing separate city districts was later expanded to include all incorporated places with populations of 200 or more. "City folks" and "country folks" could, for the first time, manage their schools in different ways.

Centralization Versus Decentralization
The last half of the 19th century witnessed a tug-of-war between the centralization and decentralization of rural school management.

Some people felt that the control of education in rural areas should be centralized in township school boards. Others believed that authority should be decentralized — that there should be sub-district (neighborhood) school boards. In 1853, the state lawmakers decided to make everybody happy and to have both township and sub-district boards.

After 40 years of bickering between the two levels, it was decided to abolish the sub-district boards. Over 33,000 sub-district board members lost their positions. This politically unpopular move was "corrected" in 1889 when sub-districts were once again authorized. Although the sub-districts were re-authorized, they were not given their former authority. For all practical purposes, the central township school boards remained in control. The township boards could, for example, confirm or reject the appointment of teachers and other employees by the sub-district boards.

The question of centralization is still with us today. There are differences of opinion, for example, concerning what the proper relationship is between (1) the central administration (board and superintendent) of a school district and (2) the staff and parents from the individual schools.

High Schools
High schools presented another problem. City school districts and a few township districts could afford them, but most of the rural districts could not. As the first century of statehood drew to a close, the *Boxwell Law* was enacted in 1892. The law was named after the state legislator who sponsored it. If a student in a district without a high school graduated from the eighth grade, he or she received a Boxwell Diploma. The rural school board was then supposed to pay tuition and send the student to a high school. However, in many cases, lack of money and transportation problems prevented the rural boards from complying with the Boxwell Law.

Samuel Lewis
Specific individuals come to mind in connection with the early

development of some aspects of local government in Ohio. For example, when considering townships, Thomas Hutchins and Thomas Jefferson come to mind; when considering counties, Arthur St. Clair; when considering council-manager municipal government, Richard Childs. Samuel Lewis holds that distinction for public schools.

Samuel Lewis, the son of a sea captain, was born in Falmonth, Massachusetts on March 17, 1799. One of nine children, he was educated at home until the family moved west to the Cincinnati area in 1813. The family moved west because the War of 1812 had brought commercial sea traffic to a near stand still.

Lewis worked as a mail carrier, as a rodman on a survey crew, and as an apprentice carpenter before he landed the job which would shape his future. While employed in the office of the clerk of courts, he decided to practice law. He did this by studying textbooks and receiving guidance from mentor lawyers. He soon became a lawyer and built a lucrative practice. He also became a licensed preacher in the Methodist Church.

Keenly aware of the value of education, he spoke and preached of the need for free common schools to enhance the opportunities of the common people. Without free common schools, he preached, "Colleges may flourish and the people be slaves." In other words, educated people may flourish but the uneducated are condemned to lives of hardship.

A new position was created by the Ohio General Assembly during its 1836–1837 session: State Superintendent of Common Schools. The position was offered to Lewis at an annual salary of $500. Despite the reduction of income, he accepted the appointment and became an able spokesman for free public education. The statistics tell the challenge he faced. In Ohio, there were 468,812 young people between the ages of four and 20. Of that total, 84,296 were in school two to four months per year and another 62,144 were in school more than four months per year. Well over 322,000 children (almost 70 percent) were receiving no schooling at all.

During his first year in office, 1837, Lewis traveled more than 1,200 miles to visit 300 schools. He traveled mostly on horseback. In his first report to the General Assembly, he observed that students needed to "learn to read, and write, and cipher according to the old standard." He also urged that sound principles of government be taught, that children should be prepared to perform the different duties of life, and that an early introduction to nature is important to popular education. He stressed the importance of having good teachers and said that the lack of good teachers "exists to a ruinous extent." He deplored the low pay of teachers and other financial problems faced by school boards. It was largely due to Lewis' first report that the state legislature levied the 1838 state tax for public education. He also recommended that county boards of education be established to supervise and assist the township boards. County boards of education, however, would not be established for another 75 years.

Free public education was not a popular political cause. It was a controversial subject and in 1839 the legislators talked of abolishing Lewis' office. He was called a "troublesome agitator" because he constantly advocated free schools, tax support, township high schools, county supervision, erection of good school buildings, teachers associations, a state university, a state normal school, free public libraries, and free educational publications.

Lewis resigned, and upon his resignation, the State Superintendent of Common Schools position was abolished. Duties of the position were transferred to the Secretary of State. Soon, the number of pupils and teachers dropped. Nevertheless, Samuel Lewis had started a fire that would not be extinguished. He remained in the public arena by repeatedly (but unsuccessfully) running for public office as a candidate for the Abolitionist Party.

One-Room School Houses

In 1915, there were 9,408 one-room elementary schools in Ohio. All but 210 were in rural areas. Today, there are none in use anywhere in the state. They were built because travel was difficult and rural homes were far apart. *Kid wagons* (the early school buses) were pulled through mud and snow by teams of horses. Inside the school house, one teacher who usually had a high school education or less taught grades one through eight. Women, by the early 1900s, were teaching in Ohio. The teacher, with the full support of parents, was the undisputed master during school hours.

One-room schools were required by state standards to have a clean building in good repair, separate screened privies for each sex or inside toilets, maps of Ohio and the United States, a library of not less than 50 books, a heating stove, windows that open, land for organized play, a certified teacher, and basic agricultural equipment. The agricultural equipment was for teaching how to farm.

One-room schools were a source of community pride and they were not given up easily. However, improved transportation, economic pressures, and the advantages of multi-room schools prevailed.

Figure 10-1: An Early Multi-Room Schoolhouse
Pupils will soon be taken home in waiting
kid wagons from this multi-room school.

Consolidation

A 1913 study by the Ohio State School Survey Commission, which was appointed by the governor, was the beginning of great changes in rural education. That study revealed the need to centralize school facilities and management. One multi-room building, for example, could replace several one-room school buildings. Larger districts could enable school boards to deal more effectively with community needs.

School buildings and management were centralized as districts were consolidated. Table 10-1 shows the number of school districts in 1913 and the number in 2001.

Table 10-1: Number of Ohio School Districts 1913 and 2001

Type of District	1913	2001
Township	1,314	0
Township Sub-District	10,120	0
Village or Special	1,280	0
City	80	191
Local	0	371
Exempted Village	0	49
Totals:	12,794	611

Public Schools Today

The Ohio General Assembly has entrusted the management and custody of the public schools to boards of education. Boards of education are also called school boards. By whatever name known, those governing boards have traditionally pursued a single purpose: to educate. That traditional role has been modified during the last few decades. School boards have been mandated to execute numerous social policies of the federal and state governments.

Each public school board is a local government with jurisdiction within its district. Boards of Education have no power of local self-government. The state legislature and the state board of education tell them what they can or must do. The ability to levy taxes subject to voter approval is an example of a *permissive* power.

State Board of Education

The Ohio Constitution provides for a state-wide public school system supervised by a state board of education. This public school system consists of two main parts: (1) the over 600 public school districts, and (2) their boards of education. State supervision is provided by setting standards, monitoring local operations, and issuing regulations. The state board oversees, among other things, curriculum, the adequacy of individual schools, changes in school district boundaries, and the distribution of state and federal funds.

The Ohio General Assembly, in 1995, increased the membership of the state board of education from 11 to 19. Eleven members are elected for overlapping four-year terms from eleven multi-county districts. Elections are non-partisan. Eight additional members are appointed for overlapping four-year terms by the governor. His appointments are subject to confirmation by the senate. Term limits are imposed by state statute. No member can serve more than two consecutive terms. To enable the board to carry out its many responsibilities, the Ohio Constitution provides for a superintendent of public instruction who serves as the chief executive officer of the Ohio Department of Education. The state board of education appoints the superintendent and the superintendent is responsible to the board.

School Districts

The township school districts which were popular in the 1800s have long since disappeared. Today, school districts are classified into general categories. This allows the General Assembly and the state board of education to deal with each group separately. Ohio school districts are classified as *city*, *exempted village*, *local*, and *joint vocational*. (In this case, the classification "local" is a name, not a description.)

A school district is the land area in which an individual school board has jurisdiction. Some districts cover an entire county while others cover only a few square miles. On a map of the state, school districts fit together like the pieces of a jigsaw puzzle. Each is a part of the state-wide school system.

School district boundaries need not follow the boundaries of any other local government. A city school district, for example, can include land outside of the city limits. District boundaries are not permanent. New districts can be created and existing districts can be consolidated. Land can be transferred from one district to another. Some changes are made to create more efficient districts, while other changes result from municipal expansion or because of the wishes of people living there.

Boundary Changes for Efficiency
Problems such as inadequate tax base, insufficient population, or failure to meet academic standards can often be solved by transferring territory or consolidating districts. Changes in district boundaries can be initiated by city, local, or exempted village boards of education, by the governing board of the county educational service center, by the state board of education, or by the residents of a district. Residents take action by filing a petition with the superintendent of the county service center. If the petition is found to be legally correct, it is certified to the county board of elections and placed on the ballot. State board resolutions which change boundaries are automatically placed on the ballot. Changes initiated by can be brought by residents of the district to a referendum vote.

Inter-District Agreements

Municipal boundaries affect school district boundaries. When *all* of the territory of a school district is annexed to a city or village, such territory becomes a part of the city school district or the school district of which the village is a part. When only a *part* of the school district is annexed, transfer of the annexed area will take place when the terms of the transfer are approved by the state board of education. State board consideration is based upon the results of negotiations between the two school boards involved. Districts involved in negotiations may agree to share tax revenues from the disputed territory, establish cooperative programs, and agree on how to settle any future boundary disputes. If the two boards cannot agree on some matters, the state board will decide the issues.

Municipal boundaries change frequently in large urban areas. In such areas, there is a central city and suburban communities which border on the central city. To encourage decision-making on the local level, state laws allows the school boards of large central city districts to enter into annexation agreements with their suburban neighbors. State law calls the central city district an *urban city district*. An urban district is defined as a city school district with an average daily attendance in excess of 20,000. An annexation agreement can provide for, among other things:

(1) Inter-district payments to compensate a district for loss of tax revenue due to participation in the agreement;

(2) Agreement that some areas will not be transferred even though annexed; and

(3) School programs which will be jointly sponsored by the two districts.

When such agreements are approved by the state board of education, the results of a proposed annexation can be determined before the annexation takes place.

✓ Did you know?

The Columbus Metropolitan Inter-District Agreement is one of the largest and most complex inter-district agreements in Ohio.

Participants include:
- Canal Winchester Local School District
- Columbus City School District
- Dublin City School District
- Franklin County School District
- Gahanna-Jefferson City School District
- Groveport-Madison Local School District
- Hamilton Local School District
- Hilliard City School District
- New Albany-Plain Local School District
- Southwestern City School District
- Westerville City School District

The current agreement is actually an extension of an understanding reached in 1986. The agreement is automatically extended every six years unless a school board elects to drop out. To date, only Reynoldsburg City School District has quit. The current extension ends June 30, 2004.

Some of the major features of the agreement are:
- Identifies suburban territories which will *not* be transferred upon annexation.
- Specifies what territories not so identified *will* be transferred upon annexation.
- Stipulates that inter-district payments will be made to compensate for revenue lost due to participation in the agreement. (2001 payments to Columbus totaled almost $5,000,000).
- Provides for jointly-operated school programs. (For example, classes for the hearing-impaired).

School Boards

County Board of Education/County Educational Service Centers
The traditional role of a county board of education was to supervise and assist the local school districts located in the county. County school boards were created in 1914 by the Ohio General Assembly. They were created to:
  (1) Centralize and consolidate rural school districts without regard to township boundaries;
  (2) Provide student transportation if the local board could not provide the service;
  (3) Supervise teacher qualification standards; and
  (4) Be the main contact with the state Board of Education.

During the 50 years following World War II, the number of Ohio school districts declined by over half. Consolidation for efficiency was largely due to the efforts of the county school boards. County boards, prior to 1995, provided supervision and management assistance to local school boards only. Also, if there was only one local school district in a county, the county board of education performed both the county and local roles. County-wide school districts are located in Adams, Hocking, Monroe, Morgan, and Vinton Counties.

A 1995 state statute provided for a change in name and duties. The name was changed to 'county educational service centers,' and the duties were broadened to benefit all public school districts. For example, what was the Franklin County Department of Education became the Franklin County Educational Service Center. Some of its activities are: curriculum development, special programs for the disabled, psychological services, and technology. Local school boards must utilize the services of their county service center. City school districts and exempted village school districts may utilize the services.

The 1995 legislation also required that county service centers with only one local district merge with a contiguous county district by July 1, 1997. In addition, any county service center that served fewer than 8,000 pupils must merge with another county service center by July 1, 1999. By 2001, mergers reduced the number of county service centers to 61.

City Boards of Education
City school boards manage districts which have a population of 5,000 or more. Some city school districts are located entirely or mostly inside a city. Others include a city, but extend far beyond the city limits. If the population falls below the 5,000 people, the city school district reverts to the *local* classification.

It is possible for a city school board to request supervision and management assistance from the county educational service center. When this happens, the city board requesting the assistance is reclassified as a local board. There are 239 cities in Ohio and only 191 city school districts. The remaining 48 city school districts have voluntarily become local school districts.

Exempted Village Boards of Education
The exempted village board of education is exempt from the supervision of the county educational service center. These boards are free of county supervision because they chose to be free. Those which existed in 1943 have been allowed to continue, but new exempted village boards cannot be created. There are 49 such boards in operation today.

If the population of an exempted village school board falls below 2,000, the district becomes a local district. If, on the other hand, the population grows to 5,000 or more, the district can become a city district.

Local Boards of Education
Most of Ohio's districts are classified as local districts. Someday, if present trends continue, there will be no exempted village school districts, only city (or urban) districts and local (or rural) districts. Urban boards will continue to be independent of county supervision and rural districts will continue to be dependent.

Joint Vocational School Districts
Any two or more school boards can develop a plan to establish a joint vocational school district. Upon approval of the plan by the

state school board, a copy of the plan is filed with each affected school board. The joint district is established when the plan receives the approval of each affected school board.

Neither the school district nor its board loses its separate identity or legal status by becoming a part of a joint vocational district. The joint district is a voluntary association of school boards.

When all participating school boards are located in the same county, the county educational service center becomes the joint vocational board of education. When the joint district crosses county boundaries, its board can be either a county board or a board composed of representatives of the participating districts. Representatives must be members of the participating boards.

Elections Below the State Level

Five members are elected on a non-partisan basis for overlapping terms of four years to serve on the governing board of a county educational service center or on the board of education of a local or exempted village district

City school elections are also non-partisan, but the size of a city board depends on the population of the district. Where the population is less than 50,000, the number of board members is not less than three nor more than five. The number of board members actually used is determined by a vote of the residents. Where the population is between 50,000 and 150,000, the board consists of not less than two, nor more than seven elected at-large, and not more than two elected from sub-districts. Exact numbers in such districts are determined by a vote of the people. Where the population is over 150,000, the board consists of between five and seven members elected at-large. Here, once again, the number actually used in each district is determined by a vote of the people.

School Management Staff

School management is unique in two respects. First, persons holding some top positions, including superintendent and principal, must hold teaching certificates. This requirement limits the field of candidates for those positions. Second, persons who perform management work are given a contract. The great majority of executives working for other kinds of local government do not have such job security.

Superintendent of Schools

The school board is responsible for the management and control of the schools. Each board appoints a superintendent to serve as its executive officer. The superintendent handles the ongoing, daily responsibilities of the board. Following the pattern established on the state level, the board appoints the superintendent and the superintendent is responsible to the board.

The superintendent of a city or exempted village school district directs and assigns teachers and other educational employees. He or she also makes pupil assignments to the various grades and schools. For local schools, these tasks are handled by the superintendent of the County Educational Service Center. A superintendent of a city or exempted village school district is not subject to the control of the county superintendent.

Business Manager

School boards may create the business manager position. The probability of finding such a position increases with the population of the school district. The larger districts have business managers while the smaller ones do not. The business manager can be made responsible to either the board or to the superintendent. He or she hires and fires non-educational employees, takes care of property, purchases supplies, and handles many other duties similar to those carried out in any business.

Treasurer

School boards must appoint a treasurer who serves as the chief financial officer for the district. The treasurer is in charge of the records and accounts of the board. In addition to fiscal responsibilities, the treasurer also serves as clerk to the board.

The Cleveland Experiment

A new kind of school district was invented in 1997. The Ohio General Assembly named it a *Municipal School District* and defined it as "a school district that is or ever has been under a federal court order requiring supervision and operational, fiscal, and personnel management of the district by the state superintendent of public instruction." In 1995, a federal judge declared Cleveland's school district, which had long been plagued by debt and low student achievement, to be in a "state of crisis" and placed it under state control. The troubled Cleveland school system had also run afoul of numerous federal social mandates. The 1997 action was taken by the state to return the school system to local control.

Following the example of other big cities (Chicago, Boston, and Baltimore) with major school problems, the Ohio General Assembly decided to place the Cleveland schools under the direction of the mayor. Why? Because there is only one mayor and the people would know exactly who is in charge. "Accountability" was the rallying cry. The new Ohio law required the mayor to appoint a nine-member school board and to hire – and have authority to fire – a chief executive officer (School Superintendent) to oversee the school system's 9,500 employees and $500 million budget. After a four-year trial period, the people of Cleveland can vote – in this case in November 2002 – on whether they wish to keep the new way of running a school system. The appointed school board took the oath of office in September 1998. Observers have concluded that the school system is now better-managed, but the Ohio Department of Education still reports a low rate of pupil academic achievement.

Paying for Ohio's Schools

The property tax has traditionally been the primary source of local revenue for public schools. As shown in Figure 10-2 below, the local share of dollars for school funding has for many years exceeded the combined amount of state and federal dollars. Thus, the burden of funding Ohio's public schools falls most heavily on the property tax.

Heavy reliance on the property tax works quite well for some school districts but not well at all for others. While local revenue per student equals over $10,000 in the richest districts, it produces less than $1,000 per student in the poorest districts. Even though each district receives a proportional share of the state and federal money, the local dollars make a tremendous difference.

Figure 10-2: School Funding Percentages
The below chart shows the share each level of government has contributed for the operation of Ohio's school since the 1959-60 school year. The state share has increased the most, but local taxes – primarily property taxes – remain the largest source of funding.

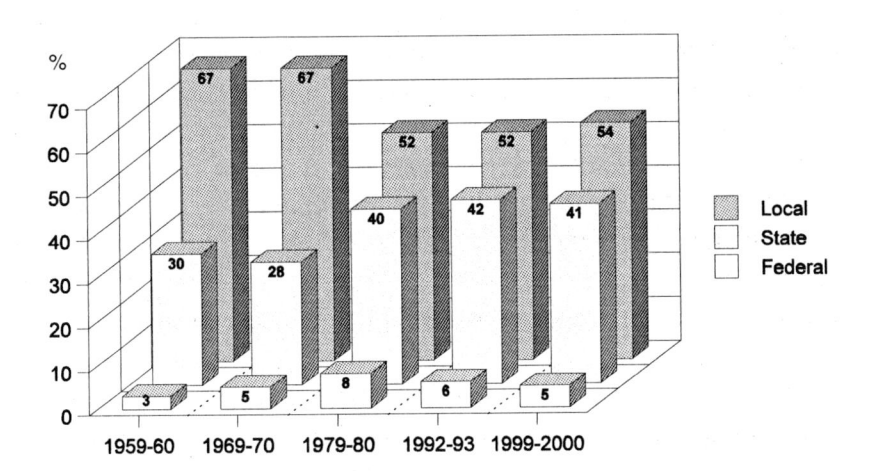

Year	Local	State	Federal
1959-60	67	30	3
1969-70	67	28	5
1979-80	52	40	8
1992-93	52	42	6
1999-2000	54	41	5

In 1995, a resident of Perry County took his concerns to the Common Pleas Court. He pointed to Section 2 of Article VI which states, in part, "The general assembly shall make such provisions, by taxation or otherwise, as . . .will secure a thorough and efficient system of common schools throughout the state. . .". The case (*DeRolph v. State of Ohio*, Case Number 1995-2066) progressed to the Ohio Supreme Court which determined that state funding does not eliminate inequities among the school districts. It instructed the General Assembly to formulate an equitable and adequate funding plan. Since 1995, two proposed plans have been developed and subsequently rejected by the Supreme Court. A third try is scheduled to be submitted on or before June 15, 2001. This matter is of higher than usual interest to students of local government not only because of the importance of adequate school funding but it is also a test of the 'separation of powers' doctrine which is so ingrained in our political science. If push comes to shove, can one branch of the state government impose its will on another?

> ✓ **Did you know?**
> The Ohio School Boards Association is a private, non-profit organization of public school boards from across Ohio. The Association's primary mission is to advance public education through the involvement and action of local citizens. To find out more about Ohio's public schools, contact:
>
> Ohio School Boards Association
> 8050 N. High Street, Suite 100
> Columbus, OH 43235
> Phone: (614) 540-4000   Website: www.osba-ohio.org

Chapter 10 Review

■ Summary

Education for the common people was not a top political priority during the early years of Ohio statehood. Teachers were paid directly by the parents of students who attended subscription schools. Land grants given by the Continental Congress to provide for public schools were mismanaged and the benefits, for all intents and purposes, were lost. It was not until 1825 that township school boards were required to levy a school tax. Even then, some school boards refused to fund more than a few months of school each year. Parents had to revert back to the subscription basis if they wanted (and could afford) additional schooling for their children. Only a few school districts had a high school. Many districts lacked the money to transport students to a high school in another district.

In 1837, there were 468,812 young people in Ohio between the ages of four and 20. Of that total, 84,296 were in school two to four months per year and another 62,144 were in school more than four months per year. Well over 322,000 children (almost 70 per cent) were receiving no schooling at all.

Samuel Lewis was appointed to the newly-created position, State Superintendent of Common Schools, in 1837. He used every opportunity available to him to advocate free schools, tax support, township high schools, county supervision, erection of good school buildings, teachers associations, a state university, a state normal school, free public libraries, and free educational publications. He more than anyone else stirred the public conscience concerning the need for free public education.

Today, the operation and management of public schools is the responsibility of school boards. The state board of education oversees the entire public school system. The role of the county boards of education (now called educational service centers) is shifting from the supervision of local districts to the support of all school districts within the county. City school boards and the boards of exempted village school districts conduct their own affairs. Two or more school boards on the local level can voluntarily form a joint vocational school district.

The size and shape of school districts is subject to change. Some change is for increased efficiency. Other change is brought about by municipal annexations. When a municipality expands, so can the school district within it. Annexations in metropolitan areas can take place frequently, and this can be disruptive to school operation. Consequently, state law allows the school boards in highly urbanized areas to enter into voluntary "annexation agreements." Such agreements can specify: (1) what territories will be transferred, (2) what territories will not be transferred, and (3) how participating school boards will be protected from financial loss due to the operation of the agreement.

All school boards employ a superintendent. The superintendent is the chief executive officer. Other executive officers are the business manager and the treasurer.

■ Glossary

Centralize. In government, to concentrate authority in a relatively few officials.

Certify. To give certain knowledge of; to attest to or vouch for.

Cipher. Arithmetic.

Common School. The term used to describe what today is known as a public school.

Curriculum. A prescribed course of study.

Decentralization. The opposite of centralization. In government, the term refers to dispersing decision-making powers throughout an organization.

Lease. A contract allowing the use of land or something else of worth for a period of time.

Normal School. A school for the teaching of high school graduates to become teachers.

Subscription School. A school wherein the teacher and parents entered into a contract for teaching services (similar to today's private schools).

Public Schools 213

Tuition. The charge or payment for instruction.

Vocation. Occupation which is not taught in colleges or universities.

■ Review Questions

1. What state agency other than the General Assembly supervises public schools in Ohio?
2. What were once named County School Boards are now named _____.
3. Below the county level, is the school board or the school superintendent responsible for the management and custody of the schools?
4. The _____ tax has traditionally been the primary source of local revenue for public schools.
5. Are school board elections partisan or non-partisan?
6. (True or false) Municipal growth in land area affects school district boundaries.
7. (True or false) Citizens can vote on school board decisions dealing with boundary changes.
8. What law enacted by the Continental Congress reserved land in the Northwest Territory for school purposes?
9. Who was the first and only Superintendent of Common Schools?
10. What is the modern equivalent of a "kid wagon?"

Answers to Review Questions: 1. State board of education; 2. Educational Service Centers; 3. School Board; 4. Property; 5. Nonpartisan; 6. True; 7. True; 8. Land Ordinance of 1785; 9. Samuel Lewis; 10. School bus.

Epilogue

The need for local government reform was obvious at the beginning of the 20th century. Large cities could not be governed and living conditions in many urban places were deplorable. Political bosses controlled. Chaotic conditions spawned a reform movement which swept the entire country. The reformers brought an end to political patronage and bossism, they gave us new forms of municipal government, and here in Ohio they gave us the ability to design our own local governments. They gave local government back to the people. Today, at the beginning of the 21st century, it is appropriate to ask, "What have we done with it?"

One thing is for certain, local governments in Ohio have flourished. We have more than 3,000 of them. The need for so many is not seriously questioned. Who would dare? There are too many defenders. The status quo is protected by thousands of present and former local government officials; each loyal to the kind of government served. Defenders are organized into statewide associations to protect their interests before the Ohio General Assembly. Some of the defenders go on to serve as members of the general assembly. Today, there are no evil political bosses to expel from power and the overwhelming majority of local governments are operated honestly. Political parties do not advocate change and the general public seems to be content with things the way they are. The subject, Local Government, is virtually ignored by the K-12 school teachers. "Why," they ask, "should we spend class time on local government when most people live in several states during their lifetime?" Local government, they point out, isn't the same everywhere. So, when it is time to teach about *community* many of them spend class time teaching their students about the Inuit (Eskimos who live in northern Alaska). Conclusion: local government flourishes in Ohio and it is well insulated from criticism or change.

Should we congratulate ourselves upon having a relatively good system of local government (as compared to 100 years ago) or should we strive for something better? What would that something better be? And, how do we bring it about? Listed below are a few troubling thoughts which can be pondered while considering those questions.

- Back in 1910, Richard Childs (see Chapter 9) cited county government as the extreme "ramshackle mechanism." In Ohio today, except for Summit County which has taken a few brave steps, that ramshackle mechanism remains basically what it was in 1910. Ohioans continue to elect three commissioners to manage some county operations and they elect eight additional chief executives to manage other parts of the county government.

- The County Home Rule Amendment to the Ohio Constitution (see Chapter 7) was adopted in 1933 and liberalized somewhat in 1957. The County Home Rule Amendment has great potential for innovative change to not only the home rule county but also to municipal and township governments which are located inside that home rule county. The possible new arrangements are literally mind boggling. Yet, repeated attempts for adoption have been beaten back by defenders of the status quo.

- Merger (see Chapters 5 and 8) allows townships and municipalities to pool their assets and to create the best possible consolidated community. This is truly a grass roots effort conducted by amateurs. The statewide associations take a 'hands-off,' neutral position and the local residents usually can't afford the services of paid consultants A nearby university might offer limited help, but all too often residents are given meager or inaccurate information concerning the anticipated consequences of merger. Most of the proposed mergers are

Epilogue

defeated at the polls. Here is another opportunity lost.

Today, we have a bloated system of local government which seems to work well enough. Although desirable changes can be identified, there is no public will to make those changes nor are there organized groups dedicated to bringing those changes about. Consequently, each person has a choice. Local government can be left in the hands of the defenders of the status quo or individual citizens can resolve to make a difference. The early 20th century reformers brought about revolution. Perhaps today, individual citizens, by staying informed and taking part, can guide the direction of evolution. It all depends on you.

Appendix:
ALL ABOUT OHIO

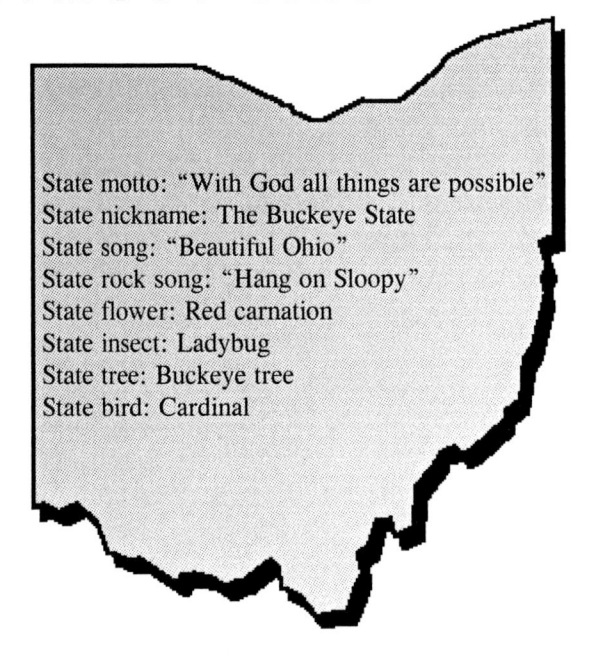

State motto: "With God all things are possible"
State nickname: The Buckeye State
State song: "Beautiful Ohio"
State rock song: "Hang on Sloopy"
State flower: Red carnation
State insect: Ladybug
State tree: Buckeye tree
State bird: Cardinal

Ohio By The Numbers

Highest point: Campbell Hill, Logan County, 1,550 feet above sea level
Lowest point: Ohio River, near Cincinnati, 433 feet above sea level
Total area: 44,828 square miles (ranks 34th among the 50 states)
Geographic center: Centerburg, Knox County
Largest county (area): Ashtabula, 711 square miles
Smallest county (area): Lake, 232 square miles
Largest county (population): Cuyahoga, 1,371,717
Smallest county (population): Vinton, 12,362

The 10 Most Populous States

(1999 U.S. Census Bureau estimates)

1. California 33,145,121
2. Texas 20,044,141
3. New York 18,196,601
4. Florida 15,111,244
5. Illinois 12,128,370
6. Pennsylvania 11,994,016
7. **Ohio** **11,256,654**
8. Michigan 9,863,775
9. New Jersey 8,143,412
10. Georgia 7,788,240

Important Dates in Ohio History

- ✓ **About 3000 B.C.** American Indians migrate to the area now known as Ohio.
- ✓ **1000 B.C.-800 A.D.** The mound builders - American Indians noted for their building of burial and ceremonial mounds - range over Ohio. Some 6,000 of the mounds remain.
- ✓ **1669-70** French explorer Robert Cavelier de La Salle explores the Ohio River area, and Louis Jolliet journeys along Lake Erie. One of them was probably the first European to set foot in Ohio. Based on La Salle's explorations and map, the French later claimed the entire Ohio Valley, a claim that was hotly disputed by the British.
- ✓ **1782** Ninety-six Delaware Indians, all of whom were Christians, are slaughtered by a posse of frontiersmen at Gnadenhutten.
- ✓ **1783** The Revolutionary War ends, and the Ohio Valley is ceded to the United States.
- ✓ **1785** With the Land Ordinance of 1785, the U.S. Congress establishes a system of gridlines for surveying the Northwest Territory, which included Ohio.
- ✓ **1787** The U.S. Congress enacts the Northwest Ordinance of 1787, which establishes a basis for the formation of six states.
- ✓ **1788** Forty-eight settlers establish Marietta, the first authorized

Appendix: All About Ohio 221

settlement in the Northwest Territory.
- ✓ **1799** Cincinnati hosts the first General Assembly of the Northwest Territory.
- ✓ **April 30, 1802** The U.S. Congress authorizes the formation of a state government for Ohio.
- ✓ **Feb. 19, 1803** President Thomas Jefferson signs a bill approving the Ohio Constitution and admitting Ohio as the 17th state. Edward Tiffin was elected the first governor, and Chillicothe was selected as the capital. The capital moved to Zanesville, back to Chillicothe, and eventually was established
in Columbus in 1816. (The U.S. Congress in 1953 discovered it had neglected to recognize Ohio's statehood officially, so it passed a resolution setting the date of Ohio's entry into the union as March 1, 1803.)
- ✓ **Sept. 10, 1813** During the War of 1812, a U.S. fleet commanded by Commodore Oliver Hazard Perry defeats the British in the Battle of Lake Erie near Put-in-Bay, Ohio. Perry announced the victory with his famous message, "We have met the enemy, and they are ours."
- ✓ **1841** William Henry Harrison, who had represented Ohio in the U.S. House and Senate, becomes the ninth president of the United States. He was the first of eight Ohioans to serve as president, but his term was cut short when he died of pneumonia a month after he insisted on delivering his lengthy inaugural address in a snowstorm, without wearing a hat or coat.
- ✓ **1851** Voters approve a new state constitution.
- ✓ **1869** The Cincinnati Red Stockings become the first pro baseball team.
- ✓ **1912** A state constitutional convention submits sweeping reform proposals to voters, who subsequently approve 33 amendments.
- ✓ **1935** A 3 percent state sales tax is enacted as the state copes with unemployment and other problems of the Depression.
- ✓ **1962** John Glenn of New Concord is the first American to orbit the Earth.
- ✓ **1969** Neil Armstrong of Wapakoneta walks on the moon.
- ✓ **May 4, 1970** Ohio National Guardsmen kill four students and wound nine others during a Vietnam War protest at Kent State University.
- ✓ **1971** State income tax adopted.
- ✓ **1995** Rock and Roll Hall of Fame opens in Cleveland; Cincinnati Reds and Cleveland Indians reach playoffs in the same year for the first time ever.

Glossary

Annex (Annexation). To combine, unite, or join together. Land can be annexed to a municipality and thus become a permanent part of the land area of that municipality. *Annexation* is the term used to refer to the procedure involved.

Annual Budget. The yearly estimates of revenues and expenditures; a plan dealing with how revenue is generated and how it is spent.

Assessed Valuation. The value placed on property for tax purposes. In Ohio, 35 percent of market value.

Bill of Rights. The first ten amendments to the U.S. Constitution. Amendments are restrictions on the federal government.

Centralize. In government, to concentrate authority in a relatively few officials.

Certify. To give certain knowledge of; to attest to or vouch for.

Charter. A document which defines how the government is organized, how its powers are distributed, and how the government operates. The charter is the basic law of the local government.

Charter Government. A government which operates according to a charter.

Cipher. Arithmetic.

City-County Consolidation. The merger of county government with other local governments within a county to form one unit of government.

City-County Separation. Political and functional separation of the city from the county. The city provides services traditionally provided by both the city and county governments.

Civil Service. A personnel system intended to hire and

protect the employment of persons selected on the basis of merit instead of political loyalty.

Commerce. The production, transportation, buying and selling of goods and services.

Commission Form of Government. A form of government in which both legislative and executive powers are exercised by a commission.

Common School. A public school.

Community. A group of people in a defined area living under common laws and rules.

Constituency. The residents of a district represented by an elective officer.

Constitution. A statement of functions and fundamental principles according to which a nation or state is governed; the supreme law of the land.

Continental Congress. The legislative and governing body of the American colonies from 1774 until 1788.

Corporation (Municipal Corporation). An artificial person created by law. As a corporation, the municipal government can function in the in the world of business.

Council-Manager Form of Government. A form of municipal government in which an elected council appoints a professional manager to administer the operational affairs of the municipality.

Curriculum. A prescribed course of study.

Debt. An obligation to return money. Local governments borrow money by issuing notes and bonds. Notes are short term debt. Bonds are long term debt. Both are formal acknowledgments of indebtedness and both promise to make payments to the note or bond holder until the indebtedness is eliminated.

Decentralization. In government, the term refers to dispersing decision-making powers throughout an organization; the opposite of centralization.

Detach (Detachment). To separate from the land area of a municipality. *Detachment* is the term used to refer to the procedure involved. The opposite of *Annex (Annexation)*.

Glossary

Election. The settling of matters by ballot.

Elector. A person who is registered to vote.

Executive Branch. That part of a governmental organization which carries out (executes) policies established by the governing body.

Federal. Pertaining to a form of government in which states have relinquished some sovereignty in order to form a union of states and a central (usually called federal) government. (In this definition, **Sovereignty** means freedom from external control).

Federalism. A system of government in which powers are divided between a central government and other (lower) levels of government. Each government is supreme within its sphere of authority. The opposite of a *unitary* system of government.

Federalists. The first American political party. It evolved during the last years of George Washington's presidency and advocated a strong central government.

French and Indian War. That part of the war between France and England (1754-1760), waged in America, in which the French received support from Native American allies. As a result of the war, France lost its claim to the Northwest Territory and other lands in North America.

Governing Body. That part of a governmental organization which establishes policy to be carried out by the executive branch.

Government. The authority to control the affairs of people living in a community.

Grant-in-Aid. A grant, usually a sum of money, by a central government to a lower level government to carry out a policy or program.

Home Rule. Self-government in local matters by a local government.

Income Tax. A tax on wages and other compensation.

Incorporation. The process by which the inhabitants of a community obtain legal status for that community and its people by forming a municipal corporation. The municipal corporation is an artificial person in the eyes of the law.

Initiative. The process by which the electorate initiates or enacts legislation. Issues are placed on the ballot by petition.

Judicial Branch. That part of a governmental organization containing one or more courts.

Justice of the Peace. A minor judge with authority to keep the peace and settle small claims cases.

Land Grant. A gift of land from the federal government to encourage development and settlement of wilderness areas.

Land Ordinance of 1785. The federal law which divided the Northwest Territory into square parts called townships. One square mile from each township was set aside to benefit schools.

Lease. A contract allowing the use of land or something else of worth for a period of time.

Legislative Branch A governing body which can enact laws; a legislature.

Legislative Process. The procedure followed by legislative bodies while enacting a law.

Lobbyist. A person who is paid by an employer to influence legislation and the decisions of public officials. Lobbyists are often referred to as the "third house" of the legislature.

Mayor-Council Form of Government. A form of municipal government in which a mayor is elected to serve as chief administrative officer and a council is elected to establish policy.

Merge (Merger). The consolidation of two municipalities or a municipality with one or more townships. *Merger* is the term used to refer to the procedure involved.

Militia. The volunteer armed forces of the states; part-time citizen soldiers.

Mill. One-tenth of a cent; a term used in reference to the property tax.

Misdemeanor. A minor criminal offense. *Misdemeanor* includes traffic violations, petty theft, disorderly conduct, gambling, and other similar offenses.

Glossary

Municipal. Pertaining to a city or village.

Nonpartisan. Not involving political parties.

Normal School. A school for the teaching of high school graduates to become teachers.

Northwest Territory. The region awarded to the United States by England in 1783, at the close of the American Revolution, extending from the Great Lakes to the Ohio River between Pennsylvania and the Mississippi River.

Open Meeting. A meeting open for attendance by persons who are not members of the group holding the meeting.

Paper Township. A township in which all township offices have been abolished. Paper townships are located inside municipal borders.

Partisan. Political; involving political parties

Patronage. The power to award employment and contracts to supporters of the political party in office.

Petition. A formal written request.

Plat. A map showing details of lots, streets, alleys, public grounds, utilities, etc.

Political Boss. A political leader who controls a state or local party organization for personal gain, not to benefit the public.

Political Machine. The party organization headed by a political boss.

Property Tax. A tax on privately-owned real estate, public utility property, and personal property (such as machinery and equipment) used in business.

Public Domain. Public lands owned by the United States government.

Public Records. Records developed and maintained by a government.

Public. The people as a whole; all of the people.

Purchasing Agent. The official in charge of buying goods, services, and equipment for a government or private business.

Referendum. The submission of a recently enacted law to a vote of the people for ratification or rejection. The process is started by petition. A *referendum* can allow voters to veto a law enacted by their legislature.

Republic. A representative democracy.

Republican. (As that term applies to Jefferson) Thomas Jefferson's political party had the name *Democrat-Republican*. The party advocated strong states and a minimal national government. It placed major emphasis on individual freedom and responsibility.

Revolution. A complete overthrow of an established government.

Sales Tax. A tax on most goods that people buy. In Ohio, medicine and uncooked foods are exempt.

Self-Government. Home rule for local affairs.

Short Ballot. A ballot listing relatively few offices and candidates for election to those offices.

Special District. A local government established to provide a single service. The service area can include one or more preexisting governments. (Also called **Special Purpose District.**)

Spoils System. The award of government jobs to political supporters and friends.

State. A sovereign political community with a distinct government which is (1) recognized as supreme by the people and (2) has jurisdiction over a given territory. In this definition, **Political** pertains to government or public, as opposed to private.

States Rights Amendment. The Tenth Amendment to the U.S. Constitution; a part of the Bill of Rights. The basic principle of U.S. federalism is fixed in the Tenth Amendment which provides that the national government is to exercise only those powers delegated to it with all other powers reserved to the states or people.

Subdivision. As used in local government, the dividing of land into building lots.

Subscription School. A school wherein the teacher and parents entered into a contract for teaching services (rather like today's private schools).

Territorial Government.

Glossary

Temporary government established by Congress to ruleuntil the Northwest Territory achieved statehood.

Tuition. The charge or payment for instruction.

Unitary System of Government. A system of government in which the central government is supreme in all matters. The opposite of *Federalism*.

Urbanization. The transformation of living conditions from rural to urban.

Vocation. Occupation which is not taught in colleges or universities.

Zoning. The designation of permissible land uses in defined areas or districts.

Index

A

Administrator (See Director of Administration)
Akron Law, 194
Andrews, Israel Ward, 21-22
Andrews, Martin, 115
Annexation
    Land transfers, 144
    Of unincorporated land, 141-142
    Procedure for, 141-142
    Proposed legislation for, 147-148, 157-161
    'Reform,' 159
    School districts, 202-203
'Annexation War of the Year 2000' (Appendix), 157-161
Archives, 64
Attorney (See Prosecuting Attorney)
Auditor
    Duties as city officer, 174
    Duties as county officer, 107

B

Bean, Roy, 66
Bill of Rights, 6-8
Blue Jacket, 100
Board of County Commissioners
    Duties of, 107-110
    Incorporation of cities and villages, 136-138
    Township boundary issues, 84-88
Board of township trustees, 76
Board of trustees of public affairs, 175
Boards of Education
    City board, 205
    County board, 204-205
    Elections, 206
    Establishment of joint-vocational school districts, 205-206
    Exempted village board, 205
    Local board, 205
    Permissive powers granted to, 200
    Quasi-corporations, designated as, 200
    Role of, 199-200
    State board, 200
Board of Zoning Appeals, 49
Bossism, 115-116, 164-165
    Conditions for bossism, 167-168
    George Cox, 116-118, 165
    Mark Hanna, 165
Boxwell Law, 195
Building Officials Conference of America (BOCA), 52

Building regulation 52-53
Burton, Harold H., 125-126

C

Canals, 67
Charter party, 118
Charters
   Adoption of, 26-28
   Charter commissions, 120
   County charters, 28
      Adoption of, 121-123
   Definition, 26
   Levying taxes, 42
   Municipal charters, 27
Childs, Richard S., 167-170
Childs, William Hamlin, 167
Cincinnati
   Boss Cox, 116-118, 165
   Municipal reform movement in, 116-118
Cities (See also Municipalities)
   Boards of Education, 205
   Classification by population, 136
   Incorporation of, 137-139
   Largest cities in Ohio (figure), 138
   Number in Ohio, 2
   Officials in, 174-175
City attorney (See Director of Law)
City auditor (See Auditor)
City clerk (See Clerk)
City commission (See Commission Form of Government)
City council
   Charter councils, 178
   Non-charter councils, 177-178

City manager (See Council-Manager)
City manager form of government, 165-166
City treasurer (See Treasurer)
City-county consolidation, 129
City-county separation, 129
Civil service commission, 175
Civil Service System
   Purpose of, 124
Civil townships (See Townships)
Clerk
   Duties as city officer, 174
   Duties as village officer, 176
Clerk of courts,
   Duties as county officer, 105
Cleveland
   Boss Mark Hanna, 165
   Cuyahoga county charter issues, 125-127
   Municipal school district, 208
Codification of ordinances, 25
Columbus Metropolitan Inter-District Agreement, 203
Commerce Clause, 8-11
Commission form of government, 166-167, 172
Commission-manager form of government, 169
Common schools (See Schools)
Communication,
   Changes in, 68
Community development director, 174
Consolidation, 86-87
Constable, 65, 77

Index

Continental Congress
  Creation of Northwest Ordinance, 95-97
  Reserving territory land for schools, 191,192
  Settlement of Northwest Territory, 59, 96
Counties
  Adoption of charters for, 121-126
  Alternate forms of government for, 127-128
  Arthur St. Clair's influence on, 97
  Boards of education (See County Educational Service Centers)
  Charters, 28
  County home rule amendment, 118-119, 127, 130
  Creation of, 19-20
  Educational Service Centers, 204-205
  Elections, 38-40
  First counties, 101-102
  Government structure of, 104-110
  Number in Ohio, 2
  Sales tax, use of, 43
  Size of, 103
Coroner
  Duties as county officer, 105
Council
  City council, 165-166
  Duties under Childs' form of government, 169
  Village council, 177

Council-manager form of government
  Childs' model of government, 169
  Differences with strong mayor form, 165-166
  Staunton experiment, 165
County auditor (See Auditor)
County clerk (See Clerk of Courts)
County commission (See Board of County Commissioners)
County home rule, 25-26
  Amendment, 118-128
County Commissioners Association of Ohio, 108
County coroner (See Coroner)
County engineer (See Engineer)
County recorder (See Recorder)
County sheriff (See Sheriff)
County surveyor (See Surveyor)
County treasurer (See Treasurer)
Court of Quarter Sessions, 21-22, 107
Courts
  County courts, 110-112
  Ohio court system, 111
Cox, George Barnesdale, 116-118, 165
Cuyahoga County
  Charter issues, 125-127

D

Davidson, Jo Ann, 160

Dayton
   Charter commission, 170, 185-189
Democracy, 28
DeRolph v. State of Ohio, 210
Detachment, 146
Director of Administration, 173-174
Director of Finance, 175
Director of Law, 175
Director of Public Safety, 175
Director of Public Service, 175

E

Education (See Schools)
Elections (See also Voting)
   General elections, 38
   Nonpartisan elections, 39
   Partisan elections, 39
   Primary elections, 38
   School board elections, 206
   Secondary elections, 38-39
Engineer
   Duties as county officer, 106-107
Executive branch
   City governments, 174-175
   County governments, 104-107
   Local governments, 37
   Village governments, 175-176
Executive sessions, 46-47
Exempted village board of education, 205

F

Fair Labor Standards Act, 9-10
Federal Department of Housing and Urban Development (HUD), 3
Federal government
   Authority over state and local governments, 4
   Duties of, 6
   Elections, 38-40
   Enforcement of federal laws, 11-15
   Establishment of, 1
   Relationship with state governments, 6-7
Federal plan, 172-173
Federalism, 4-9
   As affected by *Garcia* decision, 9-10
Federalist, The, 5-6
Federalists, 100
Fence viewer, 65, 77
Fire Chief, 176
Fire Lands Survey, 63
Fire prevention officer, 176
Franklin, Benjamin
   Ambassador to France, 62
French and Indian War, 61

G

Garcia v. San Antonio Metropolitan Transit Authority, 9-10
General Assembly (See Ohio General Assembly)
General elections
   For federal, state and county governments, 38
   For local governments, 38
General statutory forms of government, 171-172
Geographer (See United States Geographer)

Index

Grants
  Land grants, 59-60
Grants-in-aid, 11-12

H

Hamilton, Alexander, 5
Hanna, Mark, 165
High schools (See Schools)
Highway supervisor, 65, 77
Home rule
  Counties and townships, 23-24, 25-26
  County home rule amendment, 25-26, 118-119, 127, 130
  Defined, 23
  Municipal home rule, 23-24
  Township home rule, 23, 25
Hughes, Charles Evans, 9
Hutchins, Thomas, 61-63

I

Income tax, 42-43
Incorporation (See also Municipalities)
  Cities, 137-138
  Townships, 139-141
  Villages, 136-137
Indians (See Native Americans)
Initiative, 28-30
Inside millage, 41

J

Jay, John, 5
Jefferson, Thomas
  Support for civil townships, 65
  Support for Ohio statehood, 100

Jeffersonville
  Act of incorporation, 151-155
Joint-vocational school districts, 205-206
Judicial branch
  Counties, 110-112
  Local governments, 35, 37-38
Justice of the peace, 66

K

Kid wagons, 197

L

Land grants, 59-61
Land Ordinance of 1785
  Creation of, 63, 95
  Lands reserved for schools, 191, 192
  Thomas Hutchins' influence on, 62
Land use and development
  Building regulation, 52-53
  Planning, 49-50
  Subdivision regulation, 51
  Zoning, 48-49
Legislative branch
  As governing body for local governments, 33-34
  City council, 177-178
  Village council, 177
Legislative Service Commission, 147
Lewis, Samuel, 194, 195-197
Limited home rule
  Relating to counties, 25-26, 118-128
  Relating to townships, 25, 80-84

Limited self-government (See Limited home rule)
Little Turtle, 100
Local board of education, 205
Local governments
　Called "creatures of the state," 3
　Creation of, 1
　Defined, 23
　Differences among, 19
　Elections, 38-40
　Executive branch, 37
　Governing body, 35-36
　History of, 3
　Judicial branch, 37-38
　Overlapping of, 2
　Property tax, 41-42
　Services provided by, 2-3
Local self-government, 23

M

Madison, James, 5-7
Magistrate, 179
Manager (See also Council-Manager Form of Government)
　Duties under Childs' form of government, 169
Mandates, 14
Marshal, 176
Martin, Luther, 5
Mayor
　Duties under Childs' form of government, 169
　Strong mayor form, 164-165
　Weak mayor form, 164
Mayor's court, 178-180
Merger, 88-90, 145-146
Miamis (Native American tribe), 99-100
Mill, 41
Municipal home rule, 24
Municipal law, 24-25
Municipal powers, 126
Municipalities (See also Cities and Villages)
　Annexation, 141-144
　Boundary disputes with townships, 84-85
　Charters, 27
　Chief executive officer of, 163-165
　Classification of, 136-138
　Consolidation of, 86-87
　Councils, 177-178
　Detachment, 146
　Establishment of, 21
　Home rule, 23
　Income tax, 42-43
　Incorporation of, 21, 135
　Land transfer, 144
　Officials, 174-175
　Reform movements in, 115-116
　School district boundaries, effect on, 201-202
　Surrender of corporate powers, 146
　Township-municipal merger, 88-90, 145-146

N

National Road, 67
National Short Ballot Organization, 168
Native Americans
　Conflict with settlers, 99-100
　Policy of Northwest

Index

Ordinance, 99
Noble County
   Last county formed, 103
Nonpartisan, 39
Northwest Ordinance
   Creation of, 95-97
   Policy towards Native
     Americans, 99
   Provision of land for
     schools, 191
Northwest Territory
   Arthur St. Clair appointed
     governor of, 99-100
   Creation of civil townships
     in, 63-64, 65, 95
   Creation of counties in,
     20-21, 95
   Duties of territory
     governor, 20-21
   Government structure in, 96
   Land grants for settlement
     of, 59-61
   Location of, 59
   Survey of, 61

O

O'Conner, Sandra Day, 8
Ohio Basic Building Code, 53
Ohio Board of Building
   Standards, 52
Ohio City Management
   Association, 171
Ohio Company of Associates, 97
Ohio Constitution
   Allowing local-self
     government, 23-26, 118
   Creation of local
     governments, 2
   County government
     Amendments for, 128
     County home-rule
       amendment, 118-119
     Organization of, 104
   Establishment of school
     system, 200
   General statutory forms of
     government, 172
   Municipal classifications,
     establishment of, 135-136
   Optional statutory forms of
     government, 172-173
Ohio General Assembly
   Ability to change statutory
     forms of government, 173
   Ability to define local
     government powers, 2
   Annexation reform
     legislation considered,
     157-161
   Continuation of policies of
     territorial government, 96-97
   County government
     Creation of alternate
       forms for, 127-128
     Organization of, 101
   Creation of county school
     boards, 204
   Establishment of, 96, 100
   Establishment of state board
     of education, 200
   Municipalities,
     incorporation of, 135-139
   Proposed annexation
     legislation, 147-148, 157-161
   Term limits, 157-158
   Township government
     powers, 78

Ohio Historical Society, 64
Ohio Municipal League, 158, 180
Ohio Revised Code
   Accessing, 148
   Municipal corporations, 136
Ohio School Boards Association, 210
Ohio school lands program
   Land grants, 60, 194-195
Ohio Township Association, 91, 158
Open meetings, 44, 46
Optional statutory forms of government
   City manager form, 172
   Commission form, 172
   Federal plan, 172-173
Ordinance of 1787 (See Northwest Ordinance)
Ordinances, 24-25
Outside millage, 41

P
Paper townships, 85
Partial preemption, 13
Partisan, 39
Patronage, 124
Personnel Director, 175
Petitions,
   For incorporation of villages and cities, 136-138
   For initiative and referendum, 28-30
Planning, 49-50
Planning director, 174
Plat, 51
Political boss (See Bossism)
Political parties

Elections, 39
Pony Express, 68
Primary elections, 38
Property tax, 41-42
Proportional representation, 168
Prosecuting attorney, 106
Public records, 44-45
Public Records Law, 44
Public school districts (See School Districts)
Public schools (See Schools)
Putnam, Rufus, 97

Q
Quasi-corporations, 141

R
Railroads, 67
Recorder
   Duties as county officer, 106
Referendum, 28-30
Regional planning agencies, 49-50
Republic, 28
Republicans
   Ohio statehood politics, 100
   Revolt against Boss Cox, 118
Resolutions, 25, 81

S
Safety-service director, 175
Sales tax, 43
School boards (See Boards of Education)
School districts
   Boundaries, 201
   Consolidation of, 199

Index

School Districts (*Cont'd*)
Income tax, use of, 42-43
   Inter-district agreements, 202
   Joint-vocational school districts, 201
   Number in Ohio, 2
   Types of, 200-201
   Urban city district, 202
School lands program, 60, 194-195
Schools
   Akron Law, 194
   Authority of state board, 200
   Boxwell Law, 195
   Business manager, 207
   Centralization and decentralization of, 194-195, 199
   Common schools, 191
   Districts (See School Districts)
   Funding (figure), 209
   High schools, 195
   Multi-room school houses, 198
   One-room school houses, 197-198
   School system, building of, 193-194
   Subscription schools, 191-192
   Superintendent of schools, 194, 207
   Treasurer, 207-208
"Second American Revolution," 4
Seven Ranges, 62
Shawnee, 99-100

Sheriff
   Duties as county officer, 105
Solicitor, 175
Special elections, 38-39
Special purpose districts
   Definition of, 2
   Types of, 78-79
Spoils system, 116
St. Clair, Arthur
   Accomplishments in America, 98-99
   Appointed major general of Northwest Territory, 98
   Appointed territory governor, 99
   Battles with Native Americans, 99-100
   Early life, 97
   Opposition to Ohio statehood, 100-101
State government
   Establishment of, 1
States Rights Amendment, 7-8
Statutes of the State of Ohio of a General Nature, 65
Steamboats, 67
Storey, Daniel, 191
Street commissioner, 76
Strong mayor, 164-165
Subdivision regulations, 51
Subscription schools (See Schools)
Suburban Charter League, 125
Summit County
   Adoption of charter, 121-123
Sunshine Law (See also Public Records)
   Defined, 46

Executive sessions, 46-47
Superintendent of schools, 207
Supreme Court (See United States Supreme Court)
Surrender of corporate powers, 146-147
Surveying
   Ohio's major land surveys (figure), 63
   Thomas Hutchins, 60-63
   Township surveys, 63-65
Surveyor
   Duties as county officer, 106-107

T

Tammany Hall, 167
Taxes
   Income tax, 42-43
   Mill and millage, 41
   Property tax, 41-42
   Sales tax, 43
   Voter rejection of, 44
Technology
   18th and 19th century standards, 1
   Affect on civil townships, 66-68
Telegraph, 68
Tenth Amendment (See States Rights Amendment)
Term limits, 157-158
Telephone, 68
Third level (See Local Government)
Total preemption, 14-15
Township clerk, 76
Township home rule, 23, 25
Township trustees, 76

Townships
   Boundary issues, 85-90
   Civil townships
      Creation of, 65
      Decline of, 68
      Population of, 74-76
      Purposes of, 65-66, 76-78
      Technology, impact of, 66-68
   Consolidation, 86-87
   Creation of, 19-20
   Incorporation of, 139-141
   Limited self-government, 80-84
   Number in Ohio, 2
   Paper townships, 85
   Special purpose districts, 78-79
   Survey of, 63-65
   Township clerk, 76
   Township trustees, 76
   Township-municipal merger, 88-90
Transportation
   Changes in, 67
Treasurer
   Duties as city officer, 174
   Duties as county officer, 107
   Duties as village officer, 176
   School board, 207-208
   Township, 77

U

Unfunded Mandates Reform Act, 14
United States
   Creation of, 1

Index

United States Constitution
   Establishing republic form of government, 28
   History of, 28
   Ratification of, 1
United States Geographer, 60-62
United States Military District, 63
United States Supreme Court
   Role in federalism battles, 8
United States v. Lopez, 11

V

Village administrator, 176
Village clerk, 176
Village council, 177
Village treasurer (See Treasurer)
Villages (See also Municipalities)
   Classification by population, 136-137
   Incorporation of, 136-137
   Number in Ohio, 2
   Officials, 175-176
Violence Against Women Act, 11
Virginia Military District, 63-64
Voting
   Close elections (table), 40
   Eligibility, 40

W

Washington County
   First county formed, 19, 101
Washington, George
   Appointment of Arthur St. Clair as major general, 98, 100
Weak mayor, 164
Westward expansion, 1
Wilson, Woodrow, 168

Z

Zane's Trace, 60, 67
Zoning, 48-49

Acknowledgments

It is difficult to imagine a field of endeavor populated with people more dedicated to their work than those who conduct the daily business of local government. No request for assistance by the author was denied.

Appreciation is also extended to **Stephen G. Wolf** who is not only President of American Legal Publishing Corporation, but who has also served as Councilmember, City Attorney, and second-generation Mayor of the City of Mount Healthy, Ohio. Nothing would have been accomplished without the competent production oversight and editing of American Legal's **Michele Girard** (second edition) and **Rick Baltzersen** (first edition).

Long-time Maumee Solicitor (Director of Law) and former President of both the Ohio Municipal League and the Ohio Municipal Attorneys Association, **Benjamin F. Marsh**, lent his support and experience to this project. Special thanks are also extended to those who reviewed selected portions of the text: **Bruce D. McDowell**, Director, Government Policy Research, Advisory Committee on Intergovernmental Relations; **Richard A. Slee**, Deputy Director/Legal Services, Ohio School Boards Association; **Patricia Ann Taylor-Broberg**, classroom teacher and school principal, and Dr. **James B. Tinnin**, Director, the Ohio Urban University Program, Kent State University.

Photo and Illustrations Credits

Cover: Washington County Courthouse, Robb Harst

Figure 1-1: James Madison, page 5, Ohio Historical Society.
Figure 1-2: Cartoon Depiction of Partial Preemption by the Federal Government, page 13, *Columbus Dispatch*.
Figure 2-1: The Land Area of the Northwest Territory, page 20, Auditor of States' Land Office.
Figure 4-1: Ohio's Major Land Surveys, page 63, Auditor of States' Land Office.
Figure 6-1: Arthur St. Clair, page 98, Ohio Historical Society.
Figure 6-2: County Boundaries in 1797 and 1803, page 102, Auditor of States' Land Office.
Figure 6-3: Ohio Counties Today, page 103, Ohio Historical Society.
Figure 6-5: The Ohio Court System, page 111, Charles Melvin (*Ohio Government Today*).
Figure 7-1: Boss Cox, page 117, Ohio Historical Society.
Figure 8-1: Ohio's Ten Most Populous Cities, page 138, Charles Melvin (*Ohio Government Today*).
Figure 10-1: Multi-Room Schoolhouse, page 198, Ohio Historical Society.
Figure 10-2: School Funding Percentages, page 209, Charles Melvin (*Ohio Government Today*).
Appendix: All About Ohio, page 219, Charles Melvin (*Ohio Government Today*).